HOLIDAY SERMONS

A Collection of Special
Sermon Ideas from Some of
America's Best-loved Preachers

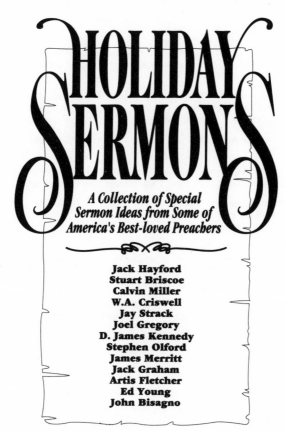

HOLIDAY SERMONS

A Collection of Special Sermon Ideas from Some of America's Best-loved Preachers

Jack Hayford
Stuart Briscoe
Calvin Miller
W.A. Criswell
Jay Strack
Joel Gregory
D. James Kennedy
Stephen Olford
James Merritt
Jack Graham
Artis Fletcher
Ed Young
John Bisagno

Edited and Compiled by Chad Brand and Clark Palmer

Thomas Nelson Publishers
Nashville·Atlanta·London·Vancouver

Published in Nashville, Tennessee, by Thomas Nelson, Inc., Publishers, and distributed in Canada by Word Communications, Ltd., Richmond, British Columbia, and in the United Kingdom by Word (UK), Ltd., Milton Keynes, England.

Unless otherwise noted, Scripture quotations are from The Holy Bible, KING JAMES VERSION.

Scripture quotations noted NKJV are from THE NEW KING JAMES VERSION of the Bible. Copyright © 1979, 1980, 1982, Thomas Nelson, Inc., Publishers.

Scripture quotations noted NIV are taken from the HOLY BIBLE, NEW INTERNATIONAL VERSION ®. Copyright © 1973, 1978, 1984 by International Bible Society. Used by permission of Zondervan Bible Publishing House. All rights reserved.

The "NIV" and "New International Version" trademarks are registered in the United States Patent and Trademark Office by International Bible Society. Use of either trademark requires the permission of International Bible Society.

Scripture quotations noted GNB are from the *Good News Bible,* Old Testament © 1976 by the American Bible Society; New Testament © 1966, 1971, 1976 American Bible Society. Used by permission.

"Cat's in the Cradle" © 1974 Story Songs, Ltd. Used by permission.

Library of Congress Cataloging-in-Publication Data

Holiday sermons : a collection of special sermon ideas from some of
   America's best-loved preachers / Jay Strack ... [et al.] ; compiled and edited
by Chad Brand and Clark Palmer.
      p.   cm.
   Includes bibliographical references.
   ISBN 0-7852-8101-0
      1. Festival-day sermons.   2. Sermons, American.   I. Brand, Chad.
   II. Palmer, Clark.
   BV4254.3.H5   1994
   252'.6—dc20   93-40292
                                                              CIP

Printed in the United States of America

1 2 3 4 5 6 7 - 00 99 98 97 96 95 94

Affectionately

dedicated to
Tina Brand
and
Yvette Palmer

Wives whose husbands rise up

to call them "Blessed"

Contents

THANKSGIVING

MOTHER'S DAY

FATHER'S DAY

INDEPENDENCE DAY

Preface

It has been estimated that John Wesley preached nearly 50,000 sermons in his lifetime. If you have been a pastor for very long, you may feel you have done at least that many. There is no denying that regular preaching and teaching take their toll on the average pastor, emotionally, spiritually, and informationally. There is a constant demand to have something to say, and if you are committed to being faithful to God and effective in your proclamation, that means having something that is *biblically sound, pastorally keen,* and something that is *fresh* and *interesting*. That's all!

The advantage we have, of course, is that the Word of God is inexhaustible. It provides ample material for years of preaching, even in the same pulpit, with little fear of retreading the same waters over and over again. However, there are those occasions in the church year when it is necessary for us to address the matters that are on the minds of our people. Most pastors follow the practice advocated by Dr. D. Martyn Lloyd-Jones of preaching appropriate messages on the great holidays of the year:

> I would lay it down as a rule that there are special occasions which should always be observed.... I believe in preaching sermons on Christmas Day and during the Advent season; I also believe in preaching special sermons on Good Friday, Easter Sunday and Whit Sunday.... Any Chris-

tian who does not respond to a sermon on the Nativity had better re-examine his whole position in Christ.[1]

These are important times and ready-made for any preacher. There is another side to this story, however.

The old preacher said, "The problem with life is that it's so *daily*." The problem with the holidays is that they are so *yearly,* and, if you consider all of them, almost *monthly.* For the "busy pastor" (and we'd like to meet one who isn't), these holidays seem to come almost *weekly.* If you pastor the same church more than a couple of years, you eventually find yourself casting around for new material to use to add sparkle and freshness to those holiday sermons. This book will become an invaluable aid in this very matter.

When the two of us began to put this material together months ago, we had several specific concerns. First, there was a decided need for *contemporary* sermons on these great holiday themes. There is no lack of older material, and much of it is still available in reprint form. Many of those older sermons are helpful and contain great insights. However, the form of preaching has undergone many changes in the last fifty years, and we saw a need for a more recent contribution.

We also felt there was a need for a book that contained material by *more than one author.* There are many extraordinary preachers in our land today, and we considered that a book that featured offerings from several of them would have a special appeal. If the single-author sermon book is like a buffet, this one is more of a potluck, but it represents the best recipe each of these verbal gourmets has to offer on the themes each was assigned. Again, this book is unique in this respect; there is no other book of holiday sermons in print by a variety of contemporary preachers.

But this is not merely a book with messages from several preachers; these men represent some of the very *best preaching* that can be heard (or read) in America today. All of them have served as pastors, though one is now a seminary professor, one is an evangelist, and two are conference speakers. These men come from a variety of denominational (and nondenominational) backgrounds. As pastors, they understand the need pastors have in the area of holiday preaching. The sermons are pastoral, warmhearted, and full of helpful illustrations and expository ideas.

We believe this book will be helpful to a variety of folks. The Sunday school teacher will find gems of information and quotable material to use in the class he or she teaches. The student will find helpful theological discussions on the doctrinal implications of these various seasons. But surely the individual who will benefit most is the "village pastor." This individual is the heart and soul of Christian ministry in America today. The one who pastors the church of average size, who maintains a small staff, and who usually does the work of two or three people will benefit most from these meditations. It is to these persons that we give our blessing and pray that the Lord will use the fruit of this labor to enhance their effectiveness in serving him.

We have learned in the past months that a project such as this requires the assistance of many hands. First, we give our thanks to the twelve preachers whose work appears in this book. To a man they extended us the courtesy of responding to our correspondence and mobilized their office personnel to help us with this project. We could have asked for no better group to work with, and we can only trust that we have rendered their creative work in an appropriate manner. Their secretaries and assistants truly demonstrated the "perseverance of the saints" in pleasantly responding to our many requests, and we thank them from the bottom of our hearts.

Our deepest debt of gratitude, however, is extended to two gems of Christian womanhood, Yvette Palmer and Tina Brand. Not only have they endured the trauma associated with the production of a manuscript such as this, but they have also patiently and constructively stood by our sides as we have labored at the task of preaching. And, whether on holiday occasions or the average Sunday, they have been a source and a resource of growth and insight as we have worked at the task of preaching the "faith which was once delivered to the saints." It is to them that this book is affectionately dedicated.

CHRISTMAS

1

The Word Made Flesh

Stuart Briscoe

M *John 1:1–14*

any people have taken great delight in studying this passage of Scripture, because it's not unlike the overture to an opera. You may not be a fan of opera—I fully realize that—but you probably rather enjoy overtures. An overture introduces all the things that are going to come in the opera. And the prologue to John's Gospel introduces you to all the themes that will be developed.

I'm sure sometimes you have grumbled about the way international news is covered. I know I have, and quite frequently. I get very frustrated when I realize that the whole of the news is going to be covered in half an hour. Because of that frustration, I'm glad we have programs such as "The MacNeil/Lehrer Report," where for an hour we have the opportunity of looking a little more fully into what is going on. It seems that many people, however, are satisfied with *slogans* and *sound bytes* rather than getting into the *substance* of what is really going on out there. It seems that, rather than take the trouble of really thinking through what is happening in the world, they want somebody else to do their thinking for them. They want someone else to come up with a capsule form and give an image of it and formulate a couple of sentences about it and perhaps a catchy slogan. That's all they want to bother themselves with. The tragedy, of course, is that then they may really possess only a very superficial understanding of the world in which they live.

It seems that this particular situation is perfectly applicable to Christmas. There is no shortage of sound bytes about Christmas. There is no shortage of superficial slogans about Christmas. I don't know how many people have wished me "Happy holiday," or how many have hoped I would have a blessed and merry Christmas. I have no idea how many people have said to me "The compliments of the season to you." All this is good and all this is proper and all this is appropriate. But is this all that Christmas is about? Are we in danger of slipping into superficial sound bytes and slogans and missing the substance of it?

The substance of Christmas is contained in this incredibly brief statement: "The Word became flesh and lived for awhile among us, and we have seen his glory." I trust that this Christmastime, while you're busy with all the other things that are a part of the Christmas experience, you will take time out to really think through the substance of what Christmas claims to be all about: The Word becoming flesh and dwelling among us. Some people who actually lived with Jesus and gazed on his glory reported what they discovered in order that we, too, might enter into their experience. The Word became flesh. I would like to share three things with you out of this brief and pungent assertion. First, I will call attention to the *recognition* of the Word, then the *revelation* of the Word, and finally I will speak to you about our *reaction* to the Word.

I fully recognize that there may be some who hear this message to whom the expression "The Word became flesh" is practically meaningless. So let me explain what the expression is really intended to convey. Let us speak of *the recognition of the Word.* You'll notice in your Bible that the word *Word* has a capital letter. That means that it is a title for something. At least that's the way it appears at first, though when you read further into the chapter you begin to discover that the *something* is actually a *Someone.* "The Word" is a title for a person. The Greek word translated "Word" is *logos.* Don't get alarmed, I'm not going to get technical at this point, but it is important that we recognize this. So what John actually said was, "The Logos became flesh."

It's rather fascinating that he used this term *logos.* You see, John was living in a world that was particularly influenced by both Greek and Hebrew thought, and the term he used to describe what he was trying to convey here was particularly relevant to both the Greeks and the Hebrews. Look at it this way: If, several years ago, I had been trying to communicate to teenagers that behind everything there was a *something* or *someone,* that things weren't superficial, but that instead there was mystery behind the whole thing, I might have gone with them to see George Lucas's *Star Wars.* I might have talked to them about "the Force," and immediately a light would have gone on in their minds. "The Force" was an expression that they were relating to. Or suppose I were to talk to a group of physicists (which would be a very dangerous thing for me to do, and I probably would never attempt it). I might discuss with them quantum theory or the idea of a unified field theory. Now, if I use the term "unified field theory" in talking to the physicists, they would know what I was talking about. On the other hand, if I were talking to some New Age people, I would have other options. They talk about things like "cosmic oneness" and such. If I were to use that language it would have meaning, and I would gain a point of reference.

Suppose for a moment that John were writing his Gospel today. If he were, I don't think he would necessarily say to his readers "the Logos became flesh." It probably wouldn't make any sense to them. He would use a term that would be familiar to New Age people or to teenagers, and while he wouldn't necessarily agree with what they mean by the term, there would be enough similarity between what they understand and how he used it for him to be able to communicate with them.

That's essentially what John did when he took the term *logos* and spoke about it in relation to Jesus. The Hebrews used to talk about God, but they were fearful of uttering his covenant name, Yahweh. The name of God was too holy to speak, and so they used other expressions in its place. There was a wide variety of them, and two of the very popular ones right about the time John was living were "Word" and "Wisdom." When the people talked about the "Word" or when they talked about "Wisdom," they were actually saying that God was the meaning behind all things. While the Hebrews were doing this the Greeks for centuries had been talking about the "Logos." When they talked about the Logos they meant something like what Heraclitus, one of their philosophers, meant—the Logos was the omnipresent wisdom by which all things were steered. The Gnostics, whose theories were beginning to develop about the time John was writing, talked about the Logos too. They believed the Logos to be the redeemer who descended into the lower world in human form, deceiving the demonic powers to make it possible for humans to follow him into the higher world of God. Now, John wouldn't have agreed with all that, but he did understand what the Greeks were thinking. They thought that behind everything there is a Reason, and the Hebrews thought that behind everything there is an Intelligence. Thus John could take both these ideas and incorporate them into the term *logos,* or *Word.*

What does he want to convey? That this Word, this Reason, this Power behind all things, this Force that is governing the universe actually existed already in the beginning. That's how John opens his Gospel: "In the beginning was the Word." Those of you who are familiar with your Bible might find a resonance there with the first verses of Genesis, the first book of the Bible. "In the beginning God created the heavens and the earth." Remember? Genesis starts with the statement about the beginning and talks about what happened at the beginning: God created. But John goes behind that and talks about *before* the beginning. This beginning that is spoken of is the beginning of the world, the universe. Genesis says that beginning came about through God acting. Yet, John says before that beginning took place the Word had already existed. That means that this Word, this Intelligence, this Force, this Power predates everything that we know, everything that we understand, everything that we can observe, everything that we can rationalize. This is what John is trying to convey.

He is also telling his people that this Word, which in the beginning had already been, was *with God.* The word that is translated "with" God is an active word that literally means "constantly face to face with God," "constantly coming toward God." The same little word is used in the story of the prodigal son who, though away from home, suddenly decides that he will return, and hurries back to be face-to-face with his father. The idea John is trying to convey is this: When the beginning of all things took place the Word had already been, eternally, and he had already been eternally at home with God, in the closest proximity with God and in the deepest intimacy with God.

Then John takes it all one step further to say, incredibly, "and the Word was God." Now notice carefully how he builds up his statement. In the beginning was the Word. The Word was with God and the Word was God. In other words, this mighty Force, this preexistent Power, this eternal Intelligence that was face-to-face with God for all eternity (before the beginning of all things) was in fact God himself. It does not say that *God was the Word,* for that would then limit God to the Word. It says, *the Word was God.* This is the first hint in John's Gospel that God exists in two Persons, and, of course, further on in chapters 14 through 17 he will make it plain that he exists in three Persons.

Furthermore, he goes on to say that the Word is also the Creator. He says it first positively, "through him all things were made," and then as if to ensure that there would be no misunderstanding, he adds the negative, "without him nothing was made that has been made" (NIV). What an incredible statement! If it is true that in the beginning the Word had already been with God and was God and he was responsible for all things being made, then it follows that matter can neither be *evil* nor *eternal*. There have always been some people (not so many nowadays, but certainly some in the days when John was writing) who have believed that matter is evil. Yet, it cannot possibly be *evil* if it was created by the eternal Word.

There are also some people who believe that matter is *eternal*. The way it is often stated today is that the universe is infinite, that it didn't have a beginning but is simply self-perpetuating. They hold that it lives in an ongoing state of regeneration, that there is a great cycle and that the universe always existed and always will go on existing. This Scripture says that cannot possibly be true because all things were made through him. This includes, of course, the material universe, but even more than that. If all things that were made were made through him, humankind was made through him too. That means that humankind can never be either *insignificant* or *independent,* for if all things that were made were made through him, *I was* and *so were you*. And if the eternal Word that existed before the beginning with God (and was God) made me and made you, don't ever let anyone convince you that you are *insignificant*. You never dare to have a low self-image, because you were created through the eternal Word, the Wisdom, and the Power and the Force eternal and divine behind all things. What an incredible compliment this is to you and to me!

Not only that. If it is true that all things that were made were made through him, including humankind, not only can we not be insignificant, but we can never be *independent* as well. We can never be what we were created to be in independence of the Force, the Power, the Intelligence that created us. This is something that our world needs to hear loudly and clearly. Augustine pointed out to us in his *Confessions* that God has made us for himself, and thus we will always be restless until we find our rest in him. This statement about the Logos says that very thing.

Now let me remind you that we're talking about Christmas. Is this your normal Christmas card stuff? Is this the kind of thing we usually chat about when we wish people the compliments of the season? I mean, do we get into this *Word* and this *eternity* thing? Do we get into the creation and the significance of humanity? Have you heard anyone on an advertisement mention the fact that human beings cannot be independent from their Creator? No! We prefer sound bytes. We prefer slogans to substance. However, the "reason for the season" (or any other cliche you like) is apparent only to those who place their lives in the hands of this very Word.

Then he pushes the matter a bit further. After making it plain that through him all things were made, he goes on to say in verses 4–5, "In him was life, and that life was the light of men. The light shines in the darkness, but the darkness has not understood it" (NIV) or "overpowered it." Now you'll find as I mentioned that the prologue is rather like the overture to an opera, introducing the themes that will be developed in the Gospel. The two most constantly recurring themes are *light* and *life*.

When John talks about *life,* he is talking about physical life; he is talking about something he calls "life to the full" and he is also talking about eternal life. This is all wrapped up in what he is saying here. This eternal Word is the source of physical life, life to the full, and eternal life. If that is true, then what people try to understand can be understood only in terms of the Logos. If they are trying to understand life, if they are trying to experience life to the full, and they want to be assured of eternal life, it's obvious where they have to start looking.

But how many people are prepared to do it? How many people are searching for fullness of life in places other than the One who in the beginning had already been in a state of eternal intimate proximity with the Father? People today are looking for fullness of life, and even life with some assurance for all time in purely material things, as opposed to spiritual realities. That's because they prefer sound bytes and slogans to substance. In him was life and this life is the light of men.

It's rather interesting to notice that John goes to great pains to say that the light goes on shining and that the darkness is not able to put it out. This probably refers to the fact that when the Lord Jesus came into the world the light of the knowledge of God had already been emanating in the world and that while darkness resists light, while all that God is has been *resisted,* while the truth that God is has been *rejected,* that does not mean that who God is and the truth that God is has ever been *obliterated.* It is true, of course, that not everyone has embraced the truth. There's no question about it that the light that comes from God through Christ the Logos shines on all, but that does not mean that all people automatically live in the good of it. The sun shines everywhere, but you can live in a cave if you wish.

In summary John is making these superlative statements and is saying that in the beginning was the Reason, the Force, the Power behind all things. That Reason is constantly in communion with God and is the source of life in every dimension. Furthermore, that Logos is the only One who can bring light into the darkness, and no darkness at all can ever overwhelm it. Now, that's all contained in this passage of Scripture, which is summarized in this brief statement, "The Word became flesh."

This brings us to the *second* point: *the revelation of the Word.* One of the most phenomenal statements that you can ever contemplate is "the Word became flesh." I'm absolutely convinced of that. Moreover, I'm absolutely convinced that our understanding of Christianity stands or falls on our understanding of this statement, "The Word became flesh." Charles Wesley was trying to wrestle with the wonder of the whole thing, and in characteristic terms he put it in one of his hymns: "God contracted to a span, incomprehensibly made man." Ask yourself a very serious substantive question this Christmas season: Do you really believe the Word became flesh? Do you really, honestly believe that God at Bethlehem was "contracted to a span, incomprehensibly made man"?

Many people who will celebrate Christmas today don't believe that. Many people want all the festivities of the holiday, but don't really believe the fundamental statement about Christmas, that what was actually happening was that God was taking the initiative and moving down into our world and assuming humanity. Now I can understand why people won't believe it. It does not *seem* logical. If he's God he's God, if he's man he's man. If he's God he can't be man, and if he's man he can't be God. That is a logically incomprehensible statement; at least, that's what many people say. To say such a thing, though, we have to assume that we know all there is to know about God and all there is to know about humans. Who could claim such a thing? We also have to assume that God couldn't do anything outside the realm of what we consider to be possible. Now, who would want to serve a God like that? There are certainly some thinkers in the church who claim that this incarnation is irrational and thus unbelievable. But this text of Scripture makes it clear that "Logos-become-flesh" is fundamental to the Christian faith. Therefore, I may have to simply accept the fact that I am confronting a mystery, but I dare not say I'm confronting a logical contradiction.

Whatever you may think about the logic of the situation, however, the real question here is "Did it happen?" I want to show you how I personally believe it is imperative that Christians believe wholeheartedly in this truth. If Jesus was just a man, a good man, a great man (somebody even goes so far as to say "the greatest man who ever lived"), then when this Jesus died on the cross it was just the death of another good man, nothing else. If just a man died on the cross, what possible good did it do? You say, "Well, he died to save us." If Jesus was just a man dying on a cross to save us, who, pray, did he save? The only person who could conceivably fit into that category is Barabbas, and Barabbas probably got himself bumped off shortly thereafter, anyway. You see, it doesn't make sense to say that something wonderful was happening on the cross if it's just a man dying there. I'm afraid that crucifixions in those days, even of good men, were a dime a dozen.

Life makes no sense without the cross, but the crucifixion makes no sense as a saving event without the incarnation. Look at it this way: One of the greatest problems people are facing in the world today is the cruelty and the horror and the violence and the sickness and the injustice of our world. Many people have become what is known as "protest atheists." These are very sensitive people. They look at the horror, the sickness, and the awfulness of this world and contend that there is absolutely no way that there can be a God who would allow all this to happen. You sometimes hear their slogans, "If 'God' is God, he's not good. If 'God' is good, he is not God."

To tell you the truth, it seems that they have a very powerful statement, unless the incarnation is true. If the incarnation is true, then God incomprehensibly became man and died on a cross. And at that particular point he did not stand with his arms akimbo watching, unconcernedly, the pains of this world, but in actual fact felt the pain of this world in its worst, most excruciating form. It may be that the protest atheists are actually going to be the people who wake up some Christian theologians and make them see that we have to stand absolutely firm on the wonder of the incarnation, if we're ever going to have anything to say to a hurting, horror-filled world. It is God in Christ, God as man dying on a cross assuming our sin who has something to offer to our world, and nobody else.

John says "we *gazed* on Him" (that's the word he uses); "we *gazed* on him, and we saw his glory." We saw the glory of his *deeds* and we saw the glory of his *words*. We saw what Jesus insisted was his moment of glorification—his death—and we were witnesses to his glorious resurrection. All of this is possible because on Christmas Day the Word became flesh. I think one of the things we may lose at Christmas time is the sense of *wonder* and accordingly a sense of *worship*. I think that it is just possible that because we don't really contemplate the wonder of the Word becoming flesh we don't really appreciate the wonder of his glory that those disciples saw. If we don't see his glory, how can we worship? We may very well trivialize Christmas even in his own house.

This brings us to the *third* and final matter, and that is *the reaction to the Word*. Notice what it says in verses 10–13: "He was in the world, and though the world was made through him, the world did not recognize him. He came to that which was his own, but his own did not receive him. Yet to all who received him, to those who believed in his name, he gave the right to become children of God— children born not of natural descent, nor of human decision or a husband's will, but born of God" (NIV). What it means simply is this: The Christ who came into the world, the Word who became flesh, incredibly, was not recognized by many, was rejected by others, and was received by some. And I can tell you that things haven't changed. There is no shortage of people today who fail to recognize what really happened in the manger. There is no shortage of people today who will accept part of what happened at Christmas but will reject Christ as their God and their only

Savior. On the other hand, there are those who gladly receive him. They are called children of God.

Notice who these children of God are. They are those who receive the Christ who died and rose again. They are the ones who affirm the incarnate Word. They receive him, and as a result, they are born of God, or born from above. I hear people today saying that they are Christians, but they don't want to be born-again Christians. I understand that born-again Christians haven't had very good press lately, and a lot of it has been well-deserved and well-earned. But if you don't want to be a born-again Christian, I'm not sure what kind you do want to be, because Scripture says that the people who have the right to be called children of God are those who are born of him, born of God.

So what it comes down to at Christmas time is asking ourselves a question. What is my response to this incredible statement that the Word became flesh? Here we celebrate the incarnation of the One who was crucified, resurrected, and glorified. What is my response to it? Have I received him? Should I not recognize him? Or do I reject him? The answer, of course, is wrapped up in this statement: "That as many as received him, that is who believed in his name, to them and to them only he gave them the right to be called children of God."

Well, I trust this will give us ample food for thought, because I'm sure we'll have ample food over the Christmas period.

2

Back to Bethlehem

Stephen F. Olford

Luke 2:1–13

*S*econd only to Jerusalem, Bethlehem is the most notable place in the unfolding drama of world events. As a city,
it has become the theme for poets, the subject for artists,
and the goal for pilgrims.

We can never celebrate Christmas without returning to
Bethlehem. As we shall see from its name and fame in
Scripture, it is a city of prophecy, history, and mystery.

Let us then come back to Bethlehem and observe, first,
that *Bethlehem is the City of Prophecy.*

> But you, Bethlehem Ephrathah,
> Though you are little among the thousands of Judah,
> Yet out of you shall come forth to Me
> The One to be Ruler in Israel,
> Whose goings forth are from of old,
> From everlasting.
>
> (Mic. 5:2 NKJV)

Without question, this is one of the clearest and most
striking messianic pronouncements. From the book of

Genesis onward we have "the prophetic word confirmed ...as a light that shines in a dark place" (2 Peter 1:19 NKJV). For example, there is that word in Eden when God said to the serpent, "I will put enmity / Between you and the woman, / And between your seed and her Seed; / He shall bruise your head, / And you shall bruise His heel" (Gen 3:15 NKJV). Then came Jehovah's promises to patriarchs, prophets, and potentates that in "the fullness of ... time" the Anointed of God would come as the wonderful "Counselor, Mighty God, / Everlasting Father, Prince of Peace" (Gal. 4:4; Isa. 9:6 NKJV). But it is generally agreed that the prophecy taught and treasured by every devout Jew was what we know today as Micah 5:2.

Here in unmistakable terms we have, first, *the identity of the coming Christ*: "But you, Bethlehem Ephrathah, / Though you are little among the thousands of Judah, / Yet out of you shall come forth to Me / The One to be Ruler in Israel ..." (Mic. 5:2 NKJV). As we shall see shortly, this One who was going to be born in Bethlehem was to be both Sovereign and Shepherd of his people. His identity is confirmed not only in the immediate context of this amazing prophecy, but also by subsequent events. You will remember that when the Magi came to Jerusalem seeking the newborn King, Herod and all Jerusalem were deeply troubled. "And when [the king] had gathered all the chief priests and scribes of the people together, he inquired of them where the Christ was to be born" (Matt. 2:4 NKJV). These doctors of the law and religious leaders, without hesitation, replied, "In Bethlehem of Judea, for thus it is written by the prophet" (Matt. 2:5 NKJV).

But more than this, we have in this prophecy *the divinity*

of the coming Christ: "Whose goings forth are from of old, / From everlasting." Here is a clear statement concerning the preexistent nature of the Babe of Bethlehem. John the evangelist affirms the same glorious truth in his prologue: "In the beginning was the Word, and the Word was with God, and the Word was God.... And the Word became flesh..." (John 1:1, 14 NKJV). Reason is baffled before the mystery of the incarnation, but what our minds cannot penetrate our hearts can reverentially and confidently accept by faith. As we behold our Lord in his eternal existence and glory, Creator of all things, Giver of life, Imparter of light, manifesting himself in all the departments of the divine operation, we bow with profoundest gratitude and holiest adoration and worship him as the Ancient of Days.

But, once again, our text reveals *the humanity of the coming Christ:* "But you, Bethlehem Ephrathah...out of you shall come forth...the One to be Ruler in Israel." This is the miracle of the Incarnation. Humans aspire; only God condescends. The Creator of all things chose to express his infinity within the confinements of a little Babe. There was no other way in which God could have spoken to us than through flesh and blood. So we read those touching and tender words: "And [Mary] brought forth her firstborn Son, and wrapped Him in swaddling cloths, and laid Him in a manger, because there was no room for them in the inn" (Luke 2:7 NKJV). God had contracted to the measure of a woman's womb. As that fully formed Babe was delivered by his mother, the first infant cry was echoed by a multitude of the heavenly host, who praised God and said, "Glory to God in the highest, / And on earth peace, goodwill toward men!" (Luke 2:14 NKJV). In that moment of time a child was born in the City of David, even a Savior who was Christ the Lord.

There is one other thought in this prophetic word which calls for comment: *the activity of the coming Christ.* "Bethlehem... out of you shall come forth... the One to be Ruler in Israel, / Whose goings forth are from of old.... And He shall stand and feed His flock / In the strength of the LORD, / In the majesty of the name of the LORD His God" (Mic. 5:2, 4 NKJV). In majestic language the messianic purpose of Christ's coming is spelled out here. Jesus came into the world to be Sovereign and Shepherd of his people. He came to be Sovereign in order to *lead* them, and he came as Shepherd in order to *feed* them with his own flesh and blood, for later he declared, "Most assuredly, I say to you, unless you eat the flesh of the Son of Man and drink His blood, you have no life in you. Whoever eats My flesh and drinks My blood has eternal life, and I will raise him up at the last day. For My flesh is food indeed, and My blood is drink indeed. He who eats My flesh and drinks My blood abides in Me, and I in him" (John 6:53–56 NKJV).

So much, then, for Bethlehem as the city of prophecy. But as we turn to the New Testament we learn, second, with equal emphasis, that *Bethlehem is the city of history.*

"Joseph [and Mary]... went up from Galilee, out of the city of Nazareth, into Judea, to the city of David, which is called Bethlehem, because he was of the house and lineage of David" (Luke 2:4 NKJV). What Micah had prophesied under the inspiration of the Holy Spirit was eventually fulfilled to the very letter. In order to grasp something of the sweep of history, gathered up in this little city of

Bethlehem, we need to consider three aspects of God's sovereign overruling of the drama of human events.

First, there is *the history of a divine preparation:* "The city of David, which is called Bethlehem..." (Luke 2:4 NKJV). In the Old Testament, we learn that Bethlehem was a town five or six miles southwest of Jerusalem, 2,500 feet above sea level in the hill country of Judea, and on the main highway to Hebron and Egypt. In Jacob's time, it was called Ephrath and was the burial place of Rachel (Gen. 35:16, 19; 48:7). After the conquest of Canaan it was called Bethlehem-judah (Ruth 1:1) to distinguish it from Bethlehem, a town of Zebulun (Josh. 19:15). It was the home of Ibzan, the tenth judge (Judg. 12:8–10); Elimelech, father-in-law of Ruth (Ruth 1:1–2); as well as her husband, Boaz (Ruth 2:1, 4). Here their great-grandson David kept his father's sheep and was anointed by Samuel (1 Sam. 17:12–15); hence it was known as "the city of David" (Luke 2:4, 11). In Jeremiah's time (41:17), the caravan inn of Chimham (2 Sam. 19:37–40) near Bethlehem was the usual starting place for Egypt. The inn mentioned in Luke 2 may have been the same place where the unborn Messiah was refused room!

We can't reflect upon this history without tracing the preparation of an all-wise God for the birth of the Savior of the world. If we examine the ancestral line through which Jesus came we shall find such names as Jacob, Boaz, Obed, Ruth, Jesse, and David—all connected with Bethlehem.

Then there is *the history of a divine visitation:* "the city of David, which is called Bethlehem...there, the days were completed for her to be delivered" (Luke 2:4, 6 NKJV). We can never read these words without being impressed with the facts that make up history. In this second chapter of Luke we read of a place, a time, and a sign that are associated with God's visitation to earth in the person of Christ.

The *place,* of course, was Bethlehem. Historians tell us that the general census that occurred at this time throughout the Roman Empire was the very first of its kind. Little did Caesar Augustus know that he was being used as the instrument for bringing about the birth of our Lord Jesus Christ in the right place. Joseph and Mary lived in Nazareth, but because the census required their presence in their ancestral home they had to make the journey to Bethlehem, in spite of Mary's condition.

What was true of the place is equally true of the *time.* If we search the pages of history we will find that in no other generation could Christ's birth have been more timely. Shakespeare once said: "There is a tide in the affairs of men." We can add to that and say there was also a tide in the affairs of God; and this was, in fact, the right moment for the coming of Christ into human history. So the angels sang: "There is born to you *this day* in the city of David a Savior, who is Christ the Lord" (Luke 2:11 NKJV, my emphasis).

But in the narrative of events there was not only a right place and time, but also a right *sign.* The angel said, "This will be the sign to you: You will find a Babe wrapped in swaddling cloths, lying in a manger" (Luke 2:12 NKJV). That sign was not a rare illusion, but a real infant wrapped in swaddling clothes, lying in a manger. So we see the reality of the divine visitation.

There is also *the history of a divine celebration:*

...the city of David, which is called Bethlehem.... Now there were in the same country shepherds living out in the fields, keeping watch over their flock by night. And behold, an angel of the Lord stood before them, and the glory of the Lord shone around them, and they were greatly afraid. Then the angel said to them, "Do not be afraid, for behold, I bring you good tidings of great joy which will be to all people. For there is born to you this day in the city of David a Savior, who is Christ the Lord."

(Luke 2:4, 8–11 NKJV)

To confirm the historic event, God ruled that there should be a threefold celebration. The immediate celebration was the appearance of an angel with the message, "'Do not be afraid, for behold, I bring you good tidings of great joy which will be to all people. For there is born to you this day in the city of David a Savior, who is Christ the Lord'" (Luke 2:10–11 NKJV). And then came "a multitude of the heavenly host praising God and saying: / 'Glory to God in the highest, / And on earth peace, goodwill toward men!'" (Luke 2:13–14 NKJV).

The subsequent celebration was that the adoration of the shepherds who, having heard the word of the angel, said:

"Let us now go to Bethlehem and see this thing that has come to pass, which the Lord has made known to us." And they came with haste and found Mary and Joseph, and the Babe lying in a manger. Now when they had seen Him, they made widely known the saying which was told them concerning this Child. And all those who heard it marveled at those things which were told them by the shepherds.

(Luke 2:15–18 NKJV)

STEPHEN F. OLFORD   **23**

Later there was the third celebration of the Magi who, having seen the star in the East, traveled many miles to Jerusalem to worship the newborn King. After making inquiries, they were led of God to a little house in Bethlehem, where they found "the young Child with Mary His mother, and fell down and worshiped Him. And when they had opened their treasures, they presented gifts to Him: gold, frankincense, and myrrh" (Matt. 2:11 NKJV). Thus we have traced briefly the history of divine *preparation, visitation,* and *celebration.*

The other thought, the third, that must be included in this Christmas meditation is the fact that *Bethlehem is a city of mystery.*

"The city of David, which is called Bethlehem..." (Luke 2:4 NKJV). It is highly significant that this city had two names—Bethlehem and Ephrathah. The name "Bethlehem" means "the house of bread," while the name "Ephrathah" means "fruitfulness" or "the fruit field." Such names in Scripture always carry divine connotations, and it does not take much research to arrive at the meanings God would have us understand and appropriate.

The Lord Jesus came into the world to be bread and wine for a fallen race. In other words, in the mystery of Bethlehem is gathered up the significance of what is meant by the body and blood of Christ. Paul expresses this thought most strikingly when he says, "Great is the mystery of godliness: God was manifested in the flesh" (1 Tim. 3:16 NKJV); or as William Hendriksen renders it: "And confessedly great is the mystery of our devotion: God [Christ] was manifest in the flesh."[1] Then follow statements that demonstrate the outworking of *Christ's devotion* to the will of God and the work of God. In other words, in order to become bread for a dying world, Jesus gave his body; and in order to become wine for that same needy world Jesus gave his blood. And the mystery or secret that can be divulged only to those who are initiates to the Christian faith, through the illumination of the Holy Spirit, is how the Lord Jesus gave his body and blood in order that he might "save His people from their sins" (Matt. 1:21 NKJV).

As we study the New Testament we learn that *the body of Christ symbolized the Savior's submission to God's redemptive will.* Jesus could say, "a body You have prepared for Me.... Then I said, 'Behold, I have come— / In the volume of the book it is written of Me— / To do Your will, O God'" (Heb. 10:5, 7 NKJV). The one consuming passion, throughout the Savior's life, was to find, follow, and finish that will. He could say, "My food is to do the will of Him who sent Me, and to finish His work" (John 4:34 NKJV). The spiritual bread on which he fed was the will of God.

If we are to know anything of the true message of Christmas, we must plumb this mystery and learn this secret of doing the will of God. Just as our Lord fed on the will of God, so must we. He could declare: "As the living Father sent Me, and I live because of the Father, so he who feeds on Me will live because of Me. This is the bread which came down from heaven.... He who eats this bread will live forever" (John 6:57–58 NKJV). This is the mystery of Bethlehem, "the house of bread." Until we make God's will the bread of our lives, we overlook the whole purpose of the incarnation.

So we see that the body of Christ symbolized the Savior's submission to God's redemptive will. But notice in the second place that *the blood of Christ symbolized the Savior's commission to God's redemptive work.* The Bible says, "Without shedding of blood there is no remission" (Heb. 9:22 NKJV). In order for that blood to be shed, however, the precious fruit of the Savior's life had to be crushed, for the Lord Jesus was not only the house of bread, he was the field of fruit. He could say: "I am the true vine, and My Father is the vinedresser" (John 15:1 NKJV). On Calvary's cross "He was wounded for our transgressions, / He was bruised for our iniquities..." (Isa. 53:5 NKJV). Because of the outpouring of his life we can now live, for Jesus declared, "My flesh is food indeed, and My blood is drink indeed" (John 6:55 NKJV). Ours is the joy to appropriate that life laid down in death and taken again in resurrection to become real in us by the Holy Spirit.

This, then, is "the mystery of godliness: God...manifested in the flesh, / Justified in the Spirit, / Seen by angels, / Preached among the Gentiles, / Believed on in the world, / Received up in glory" (1 Tim. 3:16 NKJV). As we look into the face of the Babe of Bethlehem we see there the mystery of God's redemptive will and the mystery of God's redemptive work. No wonder Simeon could hold the infant Christ in his arms and say, "Lord, now You are letting Your servant depart in peace, / According to Your word; / For my eyes have seen Your salvation" (Luke 2:29–30 NKJV).

In like manner, as we appropriate this Christ of Christmas, we shall see God's great salvation. This must be our bread and our wine. Bethlehem and Ephrathah must be more than just names; they must be a call to submission and commission in the outworking of God's saving will and work in the world today.

So as we come back to Bethlehem it is my prayer that the prophecy concerning Bethlehem will illumine us, the history of Bethlehem will inform us, and the mystery of Bethlehem will inspire us to be "broken bread and poured out wine" for needy men and women around us. Only then shall we know the true message and blessing of Christmas.

While still a young rector in Philadelphia in 1865, Phillips Brooks made a pilgrimage to Palestine. The day before Christmas he rode on horseback from Jerusalem to Bethlehem and visited the usual sights in the village, then went eastward to the traditional Field of the Shepherds. As darkness fell, he stood for a while by the cave where the shepherds saw the angels and the glory of heaven. Finally, he joined in the services conducted in Constantine's ancient basilica built in A.D. 326 over the traditional site of the nativity. The service lasted from 10:00 P.M. to 3:00 A.M. With these experiences in mind he returned to Philadelphia and wrote "O Little Town of Bethlehem," now sung all over the world. The music was composed by his organist, Lewis H. Redner, and the combined lyrics and melody exquisitely express what we mean by "back to Bethlehem."

O little town of Bethlehem, how still we see thee lie;
Above thy deep and dreamless sleep the silent stars go by.
Yet in thy dark streets shineth the everlasting light;
The hopes and fears of all the years are met in thee tonight.

For Christ is born of Mary, and gathered all above,
While mortals sleep, the angels keep their watch of wondering
    love.

O morning stars together, proclaim the holy birth;
And praises sing to God the King, and peace to all on earth!

How silently, how silently, the wondrous gift is given;
So God imparts to human hearts the blessings of his heaven.
No ear may hear his coming, but in this world of sin,
Where meek souls will receive him, still the dear Christ enters
    in.

O holy Child of Bethlehem, descend to us, we pray;
Cast out our sin, and enter in, be born in us today.
We hear the Christmas angels the great glad tidings tell;
O come to us, abide with us, our Lord Emmanuel!

3

Merry Tifton!

D. James Kennedy

2 Corinthians 9:15
Thanks be unto God for his unspeakable gift.

Even now, the echoes of Christmas are slowly fading away. That twinkling star has already disappeared from the sky, and the angelic chorus is only a faint reverberation heard over the distant Judean hills. Wait! Listen closely! Perhaps you can hear the rustle of angels' wings as they ascend back on high.

Having ripped off wrappings and bows, having examined all the neckties, perfumes, and latest in plastic aliens, some people have stood looking down at the debris scattered beneath their trees and wondered from their hearts, "Is this *all* there is to Christmas?"

We are going to address that question today through a parable I have put together for our edification. Although Jesus spun parables out effortlessly, one after another, they are anything but easy to create.

After all, a parable relates a great spiritual truth dressed in physical terms. Jesus masterfully wove the warp and woof of his parables from the things, circumstances, and events of the agrarian society his listeners lived in. Thus we read about the sheep and goats, the wheat and tares, and the son who left his father to run off into the far country. With these images, Jesus clothed his listeners' minds with understanding and moved their hearts.

In today's modern parable of Christmas, I have drawn the structure from television, because Americans spend about forty hours a week watching it, and they know it well. In particular, an old program called "The Millionaire" (a new show named "Lottery" is similar) provided some characters and details for our story. In it was a very wealthy man who would pick a person out of the blue—anybody—and give him or her $1,000,000. This wealthy man's secretary would deliver the cashier's check personally, and the program would then describe how this sudden wealth transformed the lives of its recipients.

The Legacy of Mr. Tifton

Long ago and far away, there lived a man named John Beresforth Tifton, a man whose teeming wealth stretched beyond the farthest dreams of avarice, a man in the strange habit of bestowing $1,000,000 to unsuspecting individuals of his inscrutable choice. Mr. Tifton would dispatch his secretary—Michael Anthony, replete with hat on head, umbrella under arm and briefcase in hand—to deliver not only this bountiful gift of money, but legal papers showing that the selected individual had been formally adopted into Mr. Tifton's family and given his name.

You can imagine how radically the gift transformed the

lives of its recipients. No matter what his previous financial circumstances, each individual became part of what amounted to a special millionaires' club. Receiving the name of Tifton elevated each one to a new level of prestige and respect he could never have won by himself.

First dozens, then hundreds, and finally thousands all over the world received the benefactions of Beresforth Tifton. In his will, Tifton explicitly instructed his executors that from the incalculable holdings of his vast estate this practice was to continue down through the years. Thousands upon thousands had their lives transformed as they entered the rarefied atmosphere of the millionaire.

As centuries passed, the people who had received the gift decided it would be a very good idea if they could get together in groups around the world to specially celebrate the birth of their great benefactor. They did! Remember, the only people interested in celebrating Mr. Tifton's birthday were those who had received the gift. Nobody else would have any interest in it. How could they?

As the celebrations continued and grew, Mr. Tifton had hymns written and sung to his praise, pictures drawn of him, and essays written about his character, especially his benevolence—all to honor the memory of a man who had changed untold lives.

Enter Misunderstanding

Then an unusual thing happened here in America. A few people overheard that a party was in progress. After determining its location, they went there and slipped in unnoticed. They didn't grasp what was going on, but they did pick up the idea that somebody had given wonderful gifts to these people who in turn were celebrating that deed. The party crashers thought it was a neat idea, so they told their friends, who told their friends, who told their friends, and on and on and on. Soon non-Tiftons began to celebrate Tifton's birthday too! After all, it occurred in the middle of winter, a very drab time of year, and the celebrations brightened things up a bit.

Believe it or not, the idea spread. Before long, almost everyone was celebrating Tifton Day. It is even true that Tifton Day became a national holiday. As the years rolled on, it was celebrated every year by the masses.

The department stores and other entrepreneurs, with their keen perception, liked this new holiday and were quick to put it to use for their profit. Thus they put forth their "Tifton Specials," and people bought their merchandise. Then came the Tifton card, then even the Tifton tree, though, strange to say, it did not even grow in the land of Mr. Tifton's birth.

Everywhere a Tifton

Years later, on a Tifton Eve, two gentlemen from Mr. Tifton's far-off land disembarked from a ship in New York harbor. They were genuine Tiftons, and as they walked down the gangplank, one said, "Would it not be wonderful if we could find one of the Tiftons who lives here, one who had received the gift, with whom we could celebrate our benefactor's birthday tomorrow?"

The other replied, "Ah, yes! But in such a large land as this, it is highly unlikely that in so short a period of time we should be so fortunate."

In Mr. Tifton's home country, the celebrations of his

birthday continued in their purity: Only those who had received the gift entered into them. Thus our friends were quite unprepared for what befell them.

As they walked down Fifth Avenue, they came upon a department store window that said, "Only one more day until Tifton." Their hearts leaped for joy; what good fortune they had met. Excitedly, they read another sign near the first, which said, "Tifton Specials, One-half Off!"

"We are in luck! We have found a Tifton!" one shouted gleefully to the other. "This gentleman has used his million dollars well; he has bought a department store. How strange, though, that he calls himself 'Macy's.' Americans are an odd lot."

As the two started to go into the department store to meet the owner, they heard somebody cry out from across the street, "Merry Tifton!"

Startled to find a second Tifton so soon, they turned to pinpoint the man when from their own side of the street someone cried back, "Merry Tifton to you!"

Before they knew it, a whole chorus of voices was shouting, "Merry Tifton and a Happy New Year!" The two gentlemen could hardly believe their ears. "Certainly," one said to the other, "Mr. Tifton has been very prodigal with his gifts in America, unlike anything we have ever seen in his own land." As the two gentlemen made inquiries to one person on the street, they were invited to a Tifton Eve celebration that night.

At the Tifton Eve Party

The celebration was in full swing at a large home when the two Tiftons arrived and was, in fact, a peculiarly American innovation: the Tifton Eve cocktail party. Enthusiastic before entering, they grew uneasy as they surveyed the scene inside. They heard the tinkling of glasses, raucous laughter, and music blaring through loudspeakers. Wispy clouds of smoke wafted throughout the crowded rooms. Some people were staggering about, almost falling down, because they were drunk.

The two Tiftons stood bewildered. Mr. Tifton would never have approved of this kind of conduct; it certainly did not honor his memory. This prompted one to comment, "I say, dear brother, did you notice this afternoon that some of the people who proclaimed, 'Merry Tifton' were not dressed as elegantly as one would expect?"

"Why yes, I did. I just didn't want to say anything, but they did not look like millionaires to me."

After walking around briefly, each on his own, they reunited by the fireplace and compared notes.

"You know, dear brother," one said, "I cannot begin to understand these 'Tifton cards.' Most of them do not say anything about Mr. Tifton. Instead, they show a picture of a fat man in a green suit pulled about in a chariot drawn by reindeer. What in the world has he got to do with Tifton?"

"Yes, I spoke with some people about him," the other said. "The fat man is a character that has been invented. Uriah Surper, commonly known as St. U. Surper, is his name. It's all quite confusing. We need to investigate further."

Some Astonishing Answers

They grabbed the attention of the man nearest them and asked, "Excuse us, please. Pray, tell us, sir, when did you receive your $1,000,000 from Mr. Tifton?"

"How's that?"

"I said, when did you receive your million dollars from Mr. Tifton?"

"My $1,000,000? Mac, I had to borrow $3,000 to buy my Tifton presents this year. What are you talking about?"

Our friends looked at each other and said, "Could you please tell us, then, why you are celebrating Tifton?"

"Sure! By the way, Bootstraps is the name, Benny Bootstraps. You are strangers here, too, I see. Just came from Atlanta for the holidays myself. Tifton Day, eh? Well, I'm no expert on the matter, but as I understand it, Mr. Tifton's life is written up in a big book. Most families have a copy of it in their homes, but none of them read it much. I'd like to read it more than I'm able; just don't get much time for it.

"Anyway, this book tells about the life of Mr. Tifton. He was a very rich man. I think he was from the South somewhere, maybe Dallas. He made heaps of money, and in this book he tells us how to do it. It's sort of a how-to-get-rich recipe. We are supposed to read it and apply those principles. Then, we will get rich too."

Our friends looked at each other in utter amazement, for how this explanation of Tifton Day ever cropped up was beyond them.

They continued to inquire, finding yet another man to speak to. "Excuse us, sir, but could you tell us why you are celebrating Tifton?"

"Why am I celebrating Tifton? What's the matter with you? Everybody celebrates Tifton. I've celebrated Tifton all my life. I was brought up that way. My mother celebrated Tifton, and her mother celebrated Tifton. I remember when I was just a kid, I used to hang my Tifton stocking from the mantelpiece. Why do you question our custom? Don't you have Tifton where you come from? Ours is a tradition, an old tradition, That's what it is."

Their perplexity continued, but they collared one more fellow in hope of ascertaining what Tifton Day meant to these people. "This fellow is well dressed. Perhaps he can give a sensible explanation."

"Excuse me, Mr. Tifton, my friend and I are also Tiftons, and we would like to acquire a better understanding of your celebration over here. It seems so—"

"Tifton? My name isn't Tifton. It's Mick Mythology. What a coincidence that your names are Tifton. You must get kidded a lot this time of year."

"Yes, of course," they replied. "Well, er, why do you celebrate Tifton?"

"You really don't know?"

"No, we don't."

"There was this fellow named Tifton, who lived far away and long ago. Some people claim he actually lived, but the truth is that we really don't know that. In fact, with our scientific progress and sophisticated technology, we now know that he didn't live.

"Tifton had a habit of giving presents to people—ties, handkerchiefs, cologne, and the like. It's a fable, but it's a nice idea, so we picked up on it and started giving gifts ourselves. We've changed it around a little bit, but that is basically the idea."

"So you don't really think Tifton lived and gave important gifts to people?"

"No, but like I said, it's a nice idea."

"Yes, I can see from that purple tie with the orange

stripes you are wearing," one of the Tiftons retorted, "that this is a very significant day in your life."

The Gift Unwanted

Thoroughly bewildered, the two gentlemen heard a knocking at the door. When no one answered, it opened, and through its way stepped in the perennial descendant of Michael Anthony, umbrella under one arm and briefcase in hand. The two friends from far away looked at each other with glad joy. At this party, someone was going to receive the gift. At least one person would come to know what Tifton Day was truly all about.

Mr. Anthony said, "Excuse me, please," but nobody paid him any mind; the music was so loud he could hardly be heard. Trying to talk over all the laughter and hubbub of the party, over all the tinkling of the glasses, he spoke again, "I beg your pardon, but I have here with me..." His voice was drowned out. Yet, he stepped up to the closest man, tapped him on the shoulder, and said, "Pardon me, sir, but I represent..."

The fellow interrupted, saying, "Hey, Mac, this is Tifton Eve. We don't do business on Tifton Eve. Come see me on Monday morning. Here, have a drink and celebrate. Merry Tifton to you!"

Without further ado, but dumbfounded by the disregard he received, Mr. Anthony turned and left as unnoticed as he entered. No one received the gift.

The Tifton celebration went on—undisturbed.

The Parable Explained

That is our modern parable of Christmas. How many of you who are yet weary and footsore from fighting the crowds in stores the last month have received the gift?

How many of you who have writer's cramp from authoring a hundred or more Christmas cards and are sure you will never get the taste of glue out of your mouth have received the gift?

How many of you who have finished ripping off wrappings and opening boxes but found nothing to fill your empty hearts have received the gift?

Are there any of you so spiritually benighted that you do not even know what the gift is?

Hear the words of the text for our modern parable, *"Thanks be unto God for his unspeakable gift."* That gift of God's is eternal life. That is why Jesus came. He came that we might have life, that we might have it more abundantly, that we might have it without end.

How wondrous that we should be heirs of God Almighty, that we should inherit all things. We receive his name. We are adopted into his family. We are called "Christians." That is our millionaires' club. Are you in it? You can become an heir of God and receive the gift because the New Testament of our Lord and Savior Jesus Christ is the testament of his bequeathing that gift beyond all gifts—everlasting life—to those who will trust in him. Receive that gift by acknowledging your spiritual poverty. Admit that you stand guilty before a Holy God, that you aren't a member of his family, and that you cannot lift yourself up without him. Then repent of your sins and place your trust in him who died that many might live forever.

Someone said Christ paid the debt he did not owe

because we owe a debt we could not pay. This gift was not paid for with paltry cash at a posh department store; it was paid for with the precious blood of Jesus on Calvary, a lonely hill where criminals were executed. What he has bought he stretches out his arms to offer you freely. In faith, reach out your beggar's hand to accept the gift of th King of kings.

Have you received that gift? If you have received it, then you know it. If you do not know it, it is because you have not received it. Jesus said, "Behold, I stand at the door, and knock: if any man hear my voice, and open the door, I will come in to him, and will sup with him, and he with me" (Rev. 3:20).

Please do not ignore that knock. If you do, you will have to settle for the husks of Christmas—the ribbons, the bows, the wrappings—while the water of life eludes you. You will have to be satisfied with handkerchiefs, ties, and perfume. The only thing anybody could say to you would be, "Merry Tifton."

May we pray:

O God, may no one be so blind that he cannot see how incredible is the gift which thou dost offer to us now. May those who have not received it, those who do not know they have it, and those who desire to obtain it say in their hearts right now, "O Christ, grant unto me the gift, the gift of life eternal. I do not deserve it; I never will, but I thank thee for it." Thanks be unto God for his unspeakable gift through Jesus Christ, our Lord, Amen.

4

The Three Words of Christmas

John Bisagno

John 1:1–14

It confuses me when I go to a nice restaurant and they add 15 percent to my bill. I ask the *maître d'* if that goes to the waiter, and he says, "Yes," and I ask the waiter and he says, "No." It confuses me when I'm coming into an airport, rushing to the next plane that I've just missed, and they tell me they never hold them, when I know for the last hundred trips I have sat in planes, delayed, because they were waiting for passengers from incoming planes. These things confuse me.

I don't want you to be confused about Christmas, though. This morning, as simply as I know how, I want to strip away all of the beautiful accompaniments of the Christmas story and just get to the facts. I want to make sure that you understand as succinctly and as clearly as possible the tremendous import of the three great words of Christmas: *incarnation, revelation,* and *celebration.*

First of all, let us talk about *incarnation.* This means that God himself, who is Spirit, stepped into the empirical

40

realm through the womb of the virgin and for thirty-three years revealed himself as flesh and blood in terms we can understand. He *incarnated* himself in a body that was born in a manger and lived in Nazareth, and Galilee, and died on the cross. That body, that person, is known as Jesus of Nazareth.

We cannot overstate the importance of the nature of the incarnation, for the incarnation was that miraculous event that effected the deity of Jesus on earth. And I want you to know that you can disagree about the eternal security of the believer, or the nature of baptism, or social drinking, or speaking in tongues, or any issue you wish to discuss. Those issues are *relatively* and comparatively unimportant. You cannot, however, disbelieve the incarnation and still be a true believer. You must accept and admit and confess and acknowledge and adhere to and rely on the fact that God was incarnate in Christ. He was Deity; he was humanity. Jesus was fully God and fully man, and you must confess this if you expect to be saved and go to heaven. That's as clear as I know how to make it. The deity of Jesus Christ is the watershed of Christian orthodoxy. It is no side issue; it is the issue itself.

John says it so beautifully in the prologue to his Gospel we read in our text today: "In the beginning was the Word, and the Word was with God, and the Word was God." In Greek, the expression "was with God" means to be so face to face that eyes and nose and ear and head actually become one and the same. The essence becomes the image, and the image the essence. In the beginning was the Word. In your translations, the word *word* is sometimes written with a capital W, and sometimes with a small *w.* When it is written in the lower case, it refers to the "written word" or "spoken word." When the upper case is used, the reference is to the eternal Logos, the Word that walks around in flesh. It is a Word that lives.

Now God is Spirit, and as Spirit he is invisible and cannot be seen. But once, for thirty-three years, God the Spirit chose to reveal himself in hair and skin and flesh and blood and human personality that we could identify and relate to. So when Jesus Christ came, the Word, the Essence of the Mind of God, the Logos became flesh. Jesus Christ, then, is no ambassador for God, no representative from God or spokesman about God. He is absolutely, and has always been, fully God in a human body. The Mind of God invisible is made tangible in flesh and blood, the Word made flesh.

Now the Gospels of Matthew, Mark, Luke, and John are the record of what the Word did and said, and the epistles are the theological base for the New Testament church to understand what that means for our lives. We might say that in the Bible, we have God in a book. We do not worship the Bible, of course, but in the Word of God written, in a sense we have God in a *book*. In Jesus, we have God in a *body*. In the Bible, God is on a *page;* in Jesus, God is in a *person*. In the Bible, God is on a *leaf;* in Jesus, God is in a *life*. The living Word and the printed word, then, are the twin records of God in this world.

Now, to understand the importance of Jesus as the Logos, the Word of God, the Word from God walking around incarnate in a fleshly human body, one needs to understand something of the nature of the Hebrew language. It is so powerful in its expression that, even with a limited vocabulary (only about nine hundred Hebrew words are used in the Old Testament) it makes its point pungently clear. Each of these words, then, becomes a powerful idiom for conveying truth. One simple word can conjure up ideas to an Orthodox Jew of a staggering volume of cognitive facts. To use a term coined by the famous Baptist New Testament scholar A. T. Robertson, the Hebrew language contains many "word-pictures." This idea of Jesus being the Word carries the connotation of God speaking in a life. Now the first letter of the alphabet in the Greek language is alpha; the last is omega. Jesus is called the *Alpha* and the *Omega* of God, and as such, he is the whole alphabet. He's the whole book. He's the whole chapter. He's the complete and consummate story, and everything God had to say about himself, he said in Jesus Christ. He's the Word of God living in a body.

Now the Bible makes it very clear that understanding, accepting, and believing this is essential to Christian salvation. "In him dwelleth all the fulness of the Godhead bodily" (Col. 2:9). Let me say that again: In Jesus Christ, all the fullness of God, who is a triune being, Father, Son, and Spirit, dwells bodily. How, then, can one expect to receive the Christ and subsequently in a separate act receive the Spirit of Christ? No, when you receive Jesus, you do not receive God in little bits and pieces. The fullness of God abides in him. He is the express image of the living God and to have him is to have God. He's the whole alphabet.

The Bible makes it very clear that if a person disdains that idea, rejects the idea, disbelieves the idea, and suggests that Jesus, while he was a good man, was no more than a man, that person is *not* a believer. On the contrary, he is in opposition to God. The Bible calls him an anti-Christ and a false prophet. At least three books of the New Testament were written to say primarily that the nature of the deity of Jesus effected in the incarnation through the virgin birth at Christmas is the heart of Christian orthodoxy and the watershed of the Christian faith. You must understand that he is not the one who became God, who evolved into God, who represented God, but in a way, in a mystery far past finding out, he is none other than fully God himself.

Thus *incarnation* is a great word of Christmas.

There is a *second* word that is great at Christmas—the word *revelation.* In coming into the world, God for the first and only time chose, after centuries of hiding himself, to make himself fully known to people everywhere. For millennia he had been saying, "Touch me not. You cannot look upon my face and live. Don't come too close. Take off the shoes from your feet, for you stand on holy ground." But in Christ, God came to fully reveal himself and to say, "Here is exactly what I am. The door is open; come on in and walk around." That's why John could say, "That which was from the beginning, which we have tasted and touched and handled and felt, and we make it known to you" (1 John 1:1–2). John's letter was written primarily to refute Gnosticism. The Gnostics said that all matter is evil. Therefore, Jesus could not have had a true physical body. If he had, that being matter, he would have been sinful. Therefore, Jesus Christ was a phantom. He was a ghost who existed only in the minds of the disciples. There was no real humanity, particularly in the risen Christ. This idea is still with us today, as liberal theologians contend that there was no real resurrection of a physical body from the grave. Instead, as Bultmann says, Jesus merely rose in the faith of the disciples and lives today as some power of hope for our existence. John wrote his letter to dispel such nonsense.

Jesus is the "exact representation" of the Father to humankind (Heb. 1:1-3). So, if I want to know God, I must know Jesus. If I want to ask the question "What is God like?" I must ask, "What is Jesus like?" If I want to know theological truth, moral truth, spiritual truth, I look to Christ, for he is the Authorized Revealer of the Father.

We have just finished our Christmas shopping in my house, and I hope you have. Are you satisfied with the gifts you purchased? What makes a good Christmas gift? I think the perfect Christmas gift has two qualifications. First of all, it fully represents the personality of the giver, and then it meets the need of the recipient. It represents the personality of the giver. I had the opportunity to be Chaplain to the Houston Oilers for six or seven years. The guys always were kind and courteous. One year they gave me a present, a Christmas present, that I deeply treasure. It's an autographed football. It's actually autographed, not the stamped kind that you buy at the Astrodome. All the players signed it, with a little word or a verse or something. I was so pleased and so proud of it. It was very appropriate. Suppose, however, I had received a different present, through the mail, with a card that read, "Dear Brother John, thanks a lot for the year. Here's a pair of socks we knitted just for you. Signed Earl Campbell and Dan Pastorini." I would have said something is wrong in River City. Now that's just not right. That doesn't jive.

That doesn't fit the kind of guys I know on that football team.

God sent us a Christmas gift that truly bears the stamp of the sender. God, desiring to do the one thing that would make a difference in the lives of millions of human beings, had to send someone who would truly bear his mark. He couldn't have sent a mere prophet, or a priest. He couldn't have commissioned a religious genius. The gift had to truly represent him, so he sent himself. No one but Jesus ever reflected the personality of the sender of the gift of God, thus he was the perfect Christmas gift.

An appropriate gift has another quality: It meets the need of the recipient. We needed someone who could walk where we walked, understand our rejection or embarrassment over our sins, and do something about it. We needed someone who could give us the power to overcome sin. We needed a friend who sticks closer than a brother and who could hurt as we hurt. God's gift fits.

We all get so many presents that are just not right. They are those gifts that make you want to say, "You've got to be kidding!" Like the tie a friend gave me. He gave me a knit tie. A knit tie! It's yellow and green and atrocious. Well, a lot of gifts are like that. They're good, but good for nothing. Like the little girl, who with great anticipation, opened her grandmother's long-awaited Christmas present to discover she'd sent a thimble. Well, the girl thought about it a long time. She wanted to be gracious. When she wrote to thank her grandmother, she said, "Dear Grandmother, thank you so much for the thimble. It's just what I've always wanted, but not much."

Jesus, Jesus, Jesus. Even his name tells of his ability to

meet our needs. He is the Rescuer. Is there a need he has not met? Is there a longing he cannot fill? Is there a desire in which he has not been more than adequate, sufficient? Clearly, no.

A fellow bought a new Rolls Royce. He became enamored of it. He analyzed it, read all the little books. But he couldn't find any information on the amount of horsepower the engine had, so he went back to the dealer. "I'd like to know the horsepower of my new car." The dealer chuckled, "Oh that's an old standing Rolls Royce tradition. We never divulge the horsepower of our automobiles." He thought that was cute and quaint, and went his way. But he returned a few days later and said, "You know, I've been thinking. That's a nice tradition, but it is my car. I have the right to know. I really want to know the horsepower. Tell me!" The dealer replied, "I'm sorry, sir, we have never done that. We just don't do it." Well, the man grew angry and hired an attorney and filed a lawsuit, demanding to know. The dealer finally yielded. "You be here at nine o'clock, and we'll tell you." They wired England, and there came a cablegram back. Reporters were there, the attorneys were there, and the owner of the company opened the cablegram and read it. The cable contained just one word: *adequate*. That's really all you need to know about Jesus Christ's ability to meet your every need. *He is adequate!* That's why he said, "I am. I am a friend when you're lonely. I am food when you're hungry. I am forgiveness when you're guilty. Whatever you need, just fill in the blanks." He's the great I Am. He's the revelation of God, who is adequate to our needs.

Incarnation and *revelation* are such glorious words, but there is a *third, celebration.*

What do we need more than anything in the world? They say we can live about fifty or sixty days without food, ten or twelve days without water, a few minutes without air. However, we cannot live the twinkling of an eye without hope. Somehow, someway there's got to be hope. In Manila recently, we followed the route of the Bataan Death March and viewed the island of Corregidor. There, behind the infamous walled city, we saw a prison that was not as big as our platform and choir loft, where eight hundred Filipino and British and Australian and American folks lived in 1942. They were thrown just a fragment of food once a day. There were no facilities—nothing, only bare ground, bare walls. Eight hundred people lived there, and they began to die when they gave up hope.

I don't know what the answer to the world's needs is from the world's perspective. Some think it's peace committees and peace summit meetings; others argue it is education, others material possession. Let me tell you something: That night long ago, the angels sang, "Glory to God in the highest, and on earth peace, good will toward men" (Luke 2:14).

This world is obsessed with peace. Paul Harvey said recently that of all nations represented in the UN, one hundred of the hundred and forty or fifty are at this moment either fighting themselves or fighting someone else. The world is obsessed with peace, and the Bible says that will be a characteristic of the end of time, when people will say, "Peace, peace, peace," then will come a swift and sudden destruction. But tribulation and Armageddon and the judgment of the world are but a prelude to the glorious coming of the Prince of Peace who came as a babe and who comes again as a mighty ruler. That's the Christian hope, and that's the only hope of the city and of the state and of the world, that somehow there would be peace through the Prince of Peace. That's going to happen.

Isaiah the prophet said, "The government shall be upon his shoulder" (9:6). The angel said, "of his kingdom, there shall be no end" (Luke 1:33). And we're going to see for a thousand years when Baby Jesus returns as King Jesus what this world could have been like all the time if Jesus had been Lord of every heart. That's the celebration I'm talking about today. Even at this season of hearth and home, of goodwill and smiles, it often seems there is little to celebrate. But celebration is coming!

In John, Jesus is the Creator. Did you hear it? "In the beginning was the Word, and the Word was with God, and the Word was God.... All things were made by him, and without him was not anything made that was made." The book of Genesis says, "In the beginning God created the heaven and the earth." Literally that's the expression in the Hebrew. Father, Son, and Spirit created. The Father thought it, the Son wrought it, the Spirit moved, and there was life in the world, and as the Creator and Author and Sustainer of the world, Colossians 1:17 says, "by him all things consist." That means that everything that has essence has its essence through Jesus Christ. He is the power, the force that holds it all together and gives everything cohesiveness. Peter says Jesus upholds all things by the Word of his mouth. What is the power of gravity? It's Jesus Christ. What is centrifugal force? It's Jesus Christ. In him all things hold together. He upholds all that is by the word of his mouth, and the only thing that is necessary for it all to fall apart is for him to stop speaking. When he told it to be, it was, and he says, "Continue." When he finally says, "The time is no more," it will be no more.

The beginning of the book of Revelation shows Jesus Christ with a Roman scroll at his right hand. That's the word for a title deed to a piece of property. The rest of the book tells how he unfolds it and comes back to take what is his. He created the world for God. He created it for good. He created it for our blessing. Sin has messed it up, but neither Satan nor Stalin nor Saddam Hussein nor anyone else will have the last word in history. We're moving somewhere. We're going someplace. The second coming of Jesus Christ is the central event toward which all of history is moving and without which none of history makes any sense at all. Celebrate! Rejoice, Christian! Joy to the world. The Lord has come and is coming back again.

5

Countdown to the Messiah

Jay Strack

Genesis 3:15

As we begin to celebrate this wonderful season called Christmas, as we begin to examine and anticipate all that this Christmas season actually means to us and our families in these hectic days called the nineties, let us think together about the prophecies that told of the Coming One.

There is a great deal of prophetic material in the Bible that deals with the First Advent of Jesus. The study of prophecy is fascinating in this matter of the coming of Christ. Here we can best see the divine perfection of foreknowledge and fulfillment. Because of God's omniscience, he alone can foreknow and foretell the future. And he has confined his foretelling to the pages of what is called the prophetic Word of God.

Justin Martyr, one of the Apostolic Fathers of the early church, was overwhelmed by the miracle of prophecy. He said, "To declare a thing to come to pass long before it is in being, and to work to bring it to pass: this is nothing but the supernatural work of God. Only God can do this."

As we begin to study the messianic prophecies we see

the prophets of old on tiptoes, stretching to see the birth of the Messiah, the arrival of the Anointed One. You need to know as we look at these prophecies that there are three hundred thirty-three prophecies in the Old Testament that deal with the birth and the life and the teachings and the resurrection of Jesus Christ. What better way to get caught up in the Christmas spirit than to reflect on the marvelous providence of God in foretelling the coming of Jesus Messiah! What better way to convey to our children the majesty of the season, than to reflect on the way God, in the fullness of time, sent his Son into the world!

By way of background, let us look at the *criteria for authentic prophecy.* First of all, God said in Isaiah 46:9–10, "I am God, and there is none else; I am God, and there is none like me, declaring the end from the beginning, and from ancient times the things that are not yet done, saying, My counsel shall stand and I will do all my pleasure." Then there were the words of Moses. In no uncertain terms he outlined the test of a prophet's validity. Moses said, "The prophet who presumes to speak a word in My name, which I have not commanded him to speak, or who speaks in the name of other gods, that prophet shall die. And if you say in your heart, 'How shall we know the word which the LORD has not spoken?'—when a prophet speaks in the name of the LORD, if the thing does not happen or come to pass, that is the thing which the LORD has not spoken; the prophet has spoken it presumptuously; you shall not be afraid of him" (Deut. 18:20–22 NKJV). Thus the Bible's criterion for a true prophet is 100 percent accuracy.

Jesus had the mark of a true prophet. He said in John

13:19, "Now I tell you before it come, that, when it is come to pass, ye may believe that I am he." Paul wrote that, "All scripture is given by *inspiration* of God, and is profitable for doctrine, for reproof, for correction, for instruction in righteousness: that the man of God may be perfect, thoroughly furnished unto all good works" (2 Tim. 3:16–17, emphasis mine). This word *inspiration* is the Greek word *theopneustos,* which means "the breath of God." Second Peter 1:19–21 tells us, "We have also a more sure word of prophecy; whereunto ye do well that ye take heed, as unto a light that shineth in a dark place, until the day dawn, and the day star arise in your hearts: knowing this first, that no prophecy of the scripture is of any private interpretation. For the prophecy came not in old time by the will of man: but holy men of God spake as they were moved by the Holy Ghost."

If you wish to hear the same word from the lips of Jesus, turn to Luke 24. Jesus is the fulfillment of Old Testament Scriptures. Picture the scene. Jesus has died on the cross. He shed his blood and was buried. He arose again and he is alive, making appearances to his disciples. At one of these scenes two disciples are on the road to Emmaus, and Jesus appears to them. However, they do not recognize him at first. As they tell him, somewhat incredulously, about the resurrection appearances, he laments, "O foolish ones, and slow of heart to believe in all that the prophets have spoken! Ought not the Christ to have suffered these things and to enter into His glory?" (Luke 24:25–27 NKJV). And, beginning at Moses (that is, the first five books of the Bible) and all of the Prophets (that is, Isaiah, Jeremiah, Daniel, Ezekiel, and the Minor Prophets, including Joel, Micah, and others), he preached what was surely one of the most marvelous expositions ever. He expounded to them from the Scriptures the things concerning himself. And then in verse 44 of that same chapter, Jesus went on to remind them, "These are the words which I spoke to you while I was still with you, that all things must be fulfilled which were written in the Law of Moses and the Prophets and the Psalms concerning Me" (NKJV).

Oh, my friend, please understand about the miracle of the prophecy of the Coming One. It is my prayer that as we follow the footprints of Jesus Christ through the Old Testament Scriptures, we might experience the same burning in our hearts that those disciples experienced on the road to Emmaus, when their eyes were opened and they realized that the Scriptures looked forward to and announced the arrival and even the death and resurrection of the Lord Jesus Christ.

Turn now to Genesis chapter 3. There you will find the first prophecy ever given, one that contains the first prophecy of the coming of the Deliverer, the arrival of the Savior. Now, remember there are 333 prophecies in the Old Testament that announce his coming. Jesus is the key to interpreting the Old Testament. Let me dwell on that thought for a moment. There is a story told of Harry Houdini. Many of you will recognize him as one of the greatest magicians the world has ever known. On one of his tours he put on a demonstration in Paris, trying to demonstrate his extraordinary ability to unlock any lock. He had a very sophisticated lock, which he allowed certain people to set combinations for. Then, without being told what combination they had programmed, he would "pick" the lock. What they didn't know was that there was a master combination that would unlock the lock, no matter what anyone else had programmed. However, a rival French magician who was a little upset with all the notoriety and publicity Houdini was seeming to get, announced that he could duplicate Houdini's feat, using the American's own lock. Somehow, he had obtained the secret of Houdini's trick as well as the master combination. As you would expect, Houdini was very suspicious, so he changed the master combination. Can you imagine how foolish the amateur French magician felt when in front of a large crowd he was placed in the cage, dangling above the heads of the crowd? Finally, after several hours with the crowd jeering and laughing and booing, the frustrated Frenchman finally begged Houdini to let him out. The master magician agreed, but insisted first on showing the master combination to the patient crowd. It was a five letter combination, "F-R-A-U-D." He made this magician look foolish and exposed him as a fraud.

Did you know that in like manner the One who gave us the Old Testament prophecies as a lock also knows the combination? You will never understand the Old Testament until you open that locked Old Testament using a five letter combination. The combination is "J-E-S-U-S." You see everywhere in the Old Testament Scriptures there is an air of expectancy: Someone is coming! Thus over this portion of Scripture, in fact from Genesis to Malachi, you can write one word: *expectation*. It breathes the very air of expectancy. As Old Testament scholar Walter Kaiser has reminded us, the key to the Old Testament is the word *promise*. And the key to the New Testament is *fulfillment*.[1] Even to the very last book of the Old Testament there is the lingering, looming presence of expectation, of hope. Then, when you turn the page, the Hope has been realized. The New Testament opens with the arrival or the appearance of the Expected One. You can write over the first thirty-nine books of the Bible, "expectation"; and then over the last twenty-seven books of the Bible, "manifestation." The Expected One has now arrived.

I want you to notice something as we look closely at Genesis 3:15. This verse is often called the Protevangelium, the first gospel. For us to understand Christmas, we must know that it is the fulfillment of what God began in the days of old and in times past. God created man and woman in his image, and the Bible says Adam and Eve were fellowshiping with God. They could walk with God; they could hear the voice of God. Can you imagine what a wonderful existence that must have been? But God gave Adam and Eve a choice, and they rejected the *way* of God, the *Word* of God, and the *will* of God. They were given the opportunity for eternal life, but they chose instead the way of death. And, if you read Genesis 5, which I call the graveyard chapter, you see that literally came true. It says, "and Adam died and Seth died and Lamech died and Methuselah died and everyone died except for Enoch." The first prophecy, that those who ate of the tree of the knowledge of good and evil would surely die, came true.

Then the second prophecy was voiced by God, the wonderful word of promise that predicted the Savior. What a gracious God we have! No sooner had the law of God been violated, no sooner had the ideal purpose of God been thwarted, than he made provision for the forgiveness of the lawbreakers. Verse 15 of chapter 3 informs us that God gave the first promise of the Deliverer not to Adam, not to Eve, but to the serpent, to Satan himself: "And I will put enmity [hatred] / Between you and the woman, / And between your seed and her Seed; / He shall bruise your head, / And you shall bruise His heel" (NKJV). This prophecy is given concerning the Deliverer. The Bible tells us that there was one who was to come, and he would bruise the head of Satan. At the cross of Christ, Satan tried to destroy Jesus, and thought he had. But it didn't turn out that way. Jesus was not destroyed on the cross; he was only temporarily wounded. At the cross the great enemy determined that he would beat Christ beyond recognition, that he would kill him, and so, utterly ravage God's redemptive purposes. The third-century church father Origen of Alexandria said that the devil believed the cross would be his ultimate weapon; instead it turned out to be Jesus' ultimate trophy.[2] The devil sought to destroy the Savior, but only wounded him, and in the wounding of Jesus, Satan sealed his own doom. At the cross his head was truly crushed, and his eventual destruction was certified. When Jesus died on the cross and said, "It is finished," and when he arose again from the grave, he crushed the enemy.

Not only is this the first promise of the *Savior* and the *Deliverer*, but this is also the first promise of the *virgin birth* of Christ. That phrase is very curious, "the seed of woman." Over a hundred times in the Bible there are references to "seed" and to "seeds," but it is always the "seed of man" or the "seed of mankind" that is referred to. This is the only place where the phrase "seed of woman" is used. A woman has no seed; the seed is provided by the man. But here the reference is to the seed of woman, and the only explanation is that this is a great prophecy concerning the birth of Jesus, the one who was *not* born of the seed of man, but born of a young woman who had never known a man.

Many have called this the "highway of the seed" and thus was begun the conflict of the ages. Even in the very next chapter of Genesis, chapter 4, we find the murder of Abel, where his brother Cain tried to cut off the seed line. Then the earth is filled with wickedness, with the serpent surely hoping that God would judge the planet utterly. God did judge the earth, by sending a great flood. But the enemy did not count on the grace of God, and so Noah and his family were saved, preserving a remnant, a seed. The story goes on. The family becomes a clan, a clan that goes to Egypt where they become slaves. Pharaoh attempts to eliminate the Hope by killing all the boy babies. But God raises up a deliverer, one who is a type of him who was to come. Finally, when the young virgin conceives and gives birth, another wicked king issues an edict to kill all the young male children in the vicinity. Again, God preserves his plan, and the Hope is yet preserved. This is the *highway of the seed,* and it tells us that there has been a war, a conflict down through the ages as Satan, the destroyer, has sought to parry the Lord at every turn, hoping eventually to win the conflict. Christ is the focal point of history. Even as we speak of the dates of history with reference to the birth of Jesus of Nazareth, so the great conflicts of the ages turn on the birth of the Babe of Bethlehem.

Even as all history before Christ turned on the hinge of that cow stall in Judea, so everything since the cross has pointed to another event. Just as all history before that day we call the first Christmas pointed to his first advent, so all history since then has directed our gaze to his second advent. The Bible is a mirror that both reveals and magnifies Jesus Christ. You see a threefold definition and description of Jesus in the Bible: In the Old Testament, Jesus *is coming;* in the four Gospels, Jesus *has come;* in the rest of the New Testament, Jesus *is coming again.*

The fulfillment of the promise made about the seed of the woman is also found in Galatians 3:16, 19. "Now to Abraham and his seed were the promises made. He saith not, And to seeds, as of many; but as of one, And to thy seed, which is Christ." Then why was the law given? "It was added because of transgressions, till the seed should come to whom the promise was made; and it was ordained by angels in the hand of a mediator." Then in the next chapter, Paul continues his line of thought, "But when the fulness of the time was come, God sent forth his Son, made of a woman, made under the law" (v. 4). And what does that *fullness of time* mean? This is very important, though we are able only to offer a brief summary of the implications of this phrase.

First of all, the Jews had been a chosen nation and they had given us the Old Testament. But the Jews had been spread throughout the Mediterranean world, so that by the end of the first century B.C., the promise of a Messiah from Israel was a doctrine known across the Roman Empire. This was accompanied by the influence of the Jewish belief that there was only one God, not many, as the Romans and the Greeks and the Egyptians before them had believed. Thus Jewish theology and expectation had received notice and attention in all parts of the civilized Western world. The spread of information had been facilitated by the existence of a language that had become common to all. Three centuries earlier, under Alexander the Great, the Greek culture and commerce had been introduced as a result of his successful military expansion. From that time on, the Greek tongue became the common language, the *lingua franca* of the Mediterranean world. The early Christian preaching was done in this "common Greek," and the New Testament documents were composed in the same language. The early spread of Christianity was also helped by an accomplishment of the Romans. Because of the power of Rome, internal war had virtually ceased. The peace of Rome, *pax romana,* lay on the land. It was relatively safe, then, to travel from place to place, and the early Christian missionaries benefited greatly from this, as well as from the excellent Roman system of roads, which were of such high quality that some of them still exist today. In the fullness of time the Savior has come. That phrase surely refers to all these matters, though at a more profound level, it means that the seed of the woman was born when God said that the time had come.

The prophecy had been fulfilled. It was left to the greatest of Old Testament prophets, Isaiah of Jerusalem, to give the crowning prophetic word about the event of the first Christmas. "Therefore the Lord himself shall give you a sign; Behold, a virgin shall conceive, and bear a son, and shall call his name Immanuel" (Isa. 7:14). The first chapter of Matthew records the fulfillment of that miraculous experience. The angel Gabriel informed the teenage Palestinian peasant girl that she would conceive and bear a son. When Mary wondered how such a thing could be, the heavenly visitor informed her that the Holy Spirit would come upon her and the power of the highest would overshadow her, and that the one who would be born would be called "the Son of God." So the prediction of Isaiah, made over seven hundred years earlier, was brought to pass by the power of God on that crisp evening so long ago when the angels sang, and the Hope of the world was born.

What is Christmas? It is many things, and most of them are good things. But let us never forget that it is also the evidence of promises kept—the promises of God to his people, made good in the birth of the Christ Child. "The hopes and fears of all the years are met in thee tonight."

PALM SUNDAY AND EASTER

6

The Last Week: Palm Sunday

Calvin Miller

Luke 19:37–44

The first week of April A.D. 27 was the most important week of human history! It was the final week of Jesus' life! Sunday was the day of *praise;* Thursday was the day of *trial;* Friday was the day of *dying;* Sunday was the day of *life.*

*T*here is a fickleness in the human spirit. This city that claimed Jesus as the glorious Lord on Sunday crucified him on Friday. This did not surprise Jesus, for the Bible says in John 2:25, "There was no need for anyone to tell him about them, because he himself knew what was in their hearts" (GNB). In fact, Jesus had prophesied that this is exactly how his last week would go.

In Matthew 20:18–19, before he even entered Jerusalem, he said to his disciples:

Behold, we go up to Jerusalem; and the Son of man shall be betrayed unto the chief priests and unto the scribes, and they shall condemn him to death, and shall deliver him to the Gentiles to mock, and to scourge, and to crucify him: and the third day he shall rise again.

How would you live your life? What would your behavior be if you knew you had one week to live? Jesus knew. Yet it seems all nestled together, preprogrammed for a historic finale. Beginning on Sunday with a great day of praise, Jesus came through the city gates riding on a donkey that the disciples had conveniently borrowed. The whole city broke into an anthem of blessing and praise. Those who came waved palm branches as he came. They shouted! It seemed as though they sang loud and clear, "Blessed is he who comes in the name of the Lord!"

In this exciting time there seem to surface several reasons to praise the Lord. First let us examine the *motive of expectation!*

When he came near the place where the road goes down the Mount of Olives, the whole crowd of disciples began joyfully to praise God.

(Luke 19:37*a* NIV)

Why are they praising God? They have not seen anything yet. Still, there is in the very notion of God the surge of expectancy.

We do not have to wait until God does something to praise him. We can legitimately praise him because we know he is going to do something. In the tumult of his entry, there is an expectancy! When Jesus comes into any city, that city will never be quite the same again! On any day of our lives, as we wake up, we may look to the Lord Jesus

Christ again and say, "He is my completion. I know life will be good today because Christ is good and he is in charge."

Bless God because of all you expect him to do. I still remember as a little boy when my grandmother came every year on the Frisco Railroad. She would come and we would all cluster on the front porch waiting expectantly for her. Bending our vision down those pale dust roads, we waited for that solitary figure with that marvelous carpet-bag that she always carried. And in that magic carpetbag were surprises and delights of all kinds. We carried a beautiful kind of expectancy of all that she would bring us.

In the same sense I can see these people as they cluster about the gates of the royal city! I can almost hear someone singing, "Praise God, Jesus the King is coming for me."

In the spirit of Palm Sunday, they expect the King to give them the blessings they indeed receive.

In verse 38 we are offered a second reason to praise God. "Blessed is the king who comes in the *name* of the Lord!" (Luke 19:38*a* NIV, emphasis mine).

What a wonderful name the name of the Lord is. Recently I heard two wonderful testimonies from dear friends who are facing terrible, ravaging illnesses in their bodies, reminding me that when we speak the name of Jesus over any of the conditions of life, those conditions are forced to bend to the coming of his name. Sickness, even leukemia, must bend to his wonderful name. His is ever a name of power.

I love it in *Star Wars* when R2-D2 finally spits out that little hologram of Leia. The distressed princess stands in front of Obi Wan Kenobi and says, "Help me, Obi Wan Kenobi. This is our most desperate hour."

Old Ben Kenobi looks at that little hologram standing there and says, "Obi Wan. Now that's a name I haven't heard in years!" Immediately the old man inherits a new name: With the same old system of power he has always represented, evil has a counterpart and is driven out before him as the film continues. There is power and peace in that wonderful name.

We are the people who have one name to peace. If we can stop in the most hassled moments of our lives and call on the name of Jesus, there is peace. Not long ago, vacationing in Costa Rica, our little gatekeeper told us, "I want to introduce you to somebody very important." He took us back and introduced us to a "one-half ton German Shepherd" (give or take a few kilos). And he said, "This is an important Spanish word: this dog's name is *Campion!* Can you say it?" We worked on it! "Campion!"

"When you come in here at eleven or twelve o'clock each night, it will be Campion that you meet first. You must learn to say the name of 'Campion'!"

We practiced all day long. That night when we arrived back at the gate and stuck our key in the lock, this one-half-ton dog came bounding up, snarling with his ears laid back. We gently said, "Nice doggie, Campion." (It was not too important that we could say "nice doggie" in Spanish, but it was important to be able to say "Campion.") Sure enough, just hearing his name was reassurance to Campion and, therefore, as you can imagine, a great reassurance to us.

He walked us to our room every night. We felt secure. When you have got a half-ton German Shepherd on your side in life, you have got a lot going for you!

There is power in such a name! Peace in such a name! The people who met Jesus that day said, "Blessed is he who comes in the name of power and in the name of peace." There is necessity in praising.

The Pharisees began to rebuke Jesus and said, "Do not let these people say, 'Blessed is he that comes in the name of the Lord.' They are calling you the Messiah!"

"If I rebuke them, the stones themselves would cry out," Jesus said.

I often wish Jesus had done what the Pharisees had suggested. I wish he had said, "Shame on you for calling me the Messiah. Do not ever praise me again!" And I think as that audience grew still, every little rock and pebble in the brook Kidron; every stone and boulder would have grown lips and teeth and a larynx and diaphragm and would have shouted such a resounding praise to the Lord Jesus Christ that the people's praise would have paled to insignificance.

There are *times* when God must be praised. In 1 Thessalonians 5, there are three verses that are very short. You who are opposed to scripture memory can at last bend your will; here is one you can handle. "Be joyful always" (v. 16 NIV). And if that is too long for you to memorize, try the next verse, "Pray continually" (v. 17 NIV). Then in verse 18, "Give thanks in all circumstances, for this is God's will for you in Christ Jesus" (NIV).

We must all learn to give thanks, always to be joyful!

The word *merry* is used three times in Proverbs. We do not use it much anymore, except around Christmas. But the idea is that there is a spontaneous kind of happiness that comes from the heart of the believer.

A merry heart maketh a cheerful countenance: but by sorrow of the heart the spirit is broken.

(Prov. 15:13)

Proverbs 15:15 says, "but he that is of a merry heart hath a continual feast."

If you find Jesus Christ welling up out of the spirit of your heart to praise him, you will have a continual feast! It is like a potluck that never ends. Food after food, all appending to you, all because you have a merry heart. "A merry heart doeth good like a medicine" (Prov. 17:22*a*).

In a world of glum, morose souls, I have come to love those people who have merry hearts. There are two men on the deacon council of my church in Nebraska who have merry hearts. Just to see them makes me want to laugh. I do not know what it is about them that has this effect on me. They do not seem to have any more reasons for being happy than anybody else. But every time I see them, there is this kind of grin on their faces that just causes me to break into laughter. A merry heart truly does good like a medicine! He who is merry of heart does have a continual feast! A merry heart really makes a cheerful countenance!

"Look. If I forbid these to bless me, there is a kind of spirit of joy—a merry heart that appends this universe, that puts it all together. The very rocks will give me what men themselves will not."

There is such a tendency to be caught up with those who have merry hearts, to want to join them in their merriment. Let your countenance be a continual praise unto God. Perhaps in this way we locate those who are truly experiencing Christ in life.

As he approached Jerusalem and saw the city, he wept over it.

(Luke 19:41 NIV)

What an introduction of a sour-seeming note! In the middle of all this joy, with people breaking into song around him, the Bible says Jesus wept and said to them,

If you, even you, had only known on this day what would bring you peace—but now it is hidden from your eyes.

(Luke 19:42 NIV)

Can you isolate in your own life exactly what it is that makes you receive an attitude of peace from God? What makes you feel peaceful?

It is income tax time, right? Your husband screams at you for not quite doing it like he would like you to. All of the tensions of the household get bent around getting it all paid. There is not much joy in filling out your 1040 form. You think, "Oh, if we just had more money we would have peace."

There are several little couples out here thinking, "If we could just have a house like all the other rich folks in the church, we would have peace." Is that what it takes to bring you peace? Isolate what it takes to bring you peace.

Now look at verse 43: "The days will come upon you when your enemies will build an embankment against you and encircle you and hem you in on every side" (Luke 19:43 NIV).

I want to suggest to you that what it takes to build peace in your life is not all those things that come automatically to mind. The peace point in your life relates to Jesus Christ alone: *He is peace!* Without him all these other things that you think will complete you right now will never complete you. They will be an endless agony of heart because you will be trying politically to pull in peace. You will be trying a billion things, none of which can supply it.

To build security, more is required. Jesus says to Jerusalem, "The days are coming when they are going to build an embankment around you. They are going to put a fence around you." They are going to hedge you in with difficulty, so difficult that without the fullness of Jesus Christ there is no solving it. Mark this down!

If you have not been hedged in by terror and difficulty, it is coming to you! Somewhere out there, if not right at this moment, your life will be surrounded by trials and difficulties that you cannot even imagine at this moment. Jesus said, "I weep because you do not understand the day is coming. To know the day is coming is to prepare for its coming."

Look at verse 44: "They will dash you to the ground, you and the children within your walls. They will not leave one stone on another, because you did not recognize the time of God's coming to you" (Luke 19:44 NIV). I wonder how often that is the chief sin of those who follow after Christ. We do not realize the day of God's coming unto us!

Jesus Christ proclaims himself in every circumstance of life. This is the third reason for praising in these words from Luke: *Jesus has come!* It is not as though he came to you only once—the day you received him. He comes to you every day of your life. Well, why then do you not see him every day? Because you are busy. Because you get up and run to this meeting or that. You have a million things to do. Some of them even go under the name "spiritual."

You run to this church until you are out of breath, as though this is all of life. But do not be deceived. There is never any life in running.

Life is in Jesus Christ alone, in his person. And the smart person learns to recognize the moment of the coming of Jesus Christ. I have this fear that in my most desperate moments, my own grief gets between me and the Lord. At such moments, he comes to me. But I am so self-concerned and wrapped up in the littleness that is myself that I cannot see the greatness that is him.

"I weep because you did not recognize the day of my coming," cried the Christ. You see what is happening? Man, they are crowding the streets. Jesus is on the donkey. They throw clothes in his way! They shout and they cheer! Jesus is coming! And he is weeping. "I am coming to you and you are rejecting me. Indeed, you will kill me."

I have often wondered what makes us think, as Christians, that we will be so eager to see Jesus in eternity when we have been so "uneager" to see him in the present moment! We think that someday, all of a sudden, we are going to burst into song when we see him in all his glory. But will it be so for those of us who have feared him, run from him, avoided him in this life?

From day to day we miss the moments of his coming. He wants a little time with us, and we do not have it. We are too busy! He wants us to stop a moment and cry in his presence, or laugh with him, or sit with him at that wonderful table in the wilderness.

What is the point? Praise and blessing must become a part of our lives. If we have that merry heart, it will be because we have understood that the Lord Jesus Christ is regular in his coming to us and invites us to walk with him and to celebrate him every moment.

Then every morning can be like this Palm Sunday celebration in your life—every morning a celebration of His Lordship.

To wait in such expectancy is to know in joy the moment of his coming.

7

Unshakable Facts in a Shaky World

Jack Hayford

Acts 1:1–3

The former account I made, O Theophilus, of all that Jesus began both to do and teach, until the day in which He was taken up, after He through the Holy Spirit had given commandments to the apostles whom He had chosen, to whom He also presented Himself alive after His suffering by many infallible proofs, being seen by them during forty days and speaking of the things pertaining to the kingdom of God.

(Acts 1:1–3 NKJV)

*L*ook at that phrase, "many infallible proofs." I want to talk to you about the *live-ability* of the resurrection. "Because I live, you too shall live," Jesus says. I want to talk also about the *credibility* of the resurrection, its believe-ability. There is every reason to know with certainty that we are dealing not with a mystery, not with a phantom, not with imagination or poetry. We are not dealing with some ectoplasmic formation that simply conjured itself and made a presentation. Jesus presented *himself* alive to his disciples.

These words in Acts are written by one of the most respected historians from antiquity, not respected because he wrote in the Bible, but respected by people who critique ancient literature. Literary critics do this, and if you want to study it in detail there is plenty of material out there in the libraries. These critics read and study the writings of an author from antiquity and determine the different hallmarks of his writing, not so much the style, but the facts that he relates. They investigate whether they're traceable to verifiable data that are from that same era by other authors, and that's the way they verify the trustworthiness of the historian. Luke was a physician, a scientist, a trusted historian, and to this day he is one of the most respected ones from antiquity.

In the book of Acts he says, "I wrote to you a former treatise, Theophilus..." He's addressing a specific person. The former treatise he is referring to is the Gospel of Luke, which he also wrote. And he says there were many infallible proofs. This is important to a scientific mind, and being a doctor, it's the way he thinks. So there is inescapable evidence. That evidence is measurable.

My purpose is not to elaborate at length on the *credible* evidence of Jesus' resurrection. I do want to say a few words around about it, though, because it is important. Most of us gathered today don't need anybody to prove to us that Jesus is risen from the dead. We're like the songwriter who penned, "You ask me how I know He lives? He lives within my heart." Most of us would say "Hallelujah" to that. That's true. You know that. But until you've had your own living encounter with Jesus Christ, the starting point is to come to terms with the fact that there is stark, raw evidence that is there. Measurable! Inescapable! You can refuse it. You can deny it. You can close the door on it. You can play ostrich games with it, but that's not going to make it go away. It's factual.

Amazing numbers of Christians who believe in Jesus don't know the incredible body of evidence concerning his resurrection. Let me just illustrate it. Suppose we just vacate a large portion of our auditorium today, and then bring in from history every one of the people who literally, physically saw the risen Jesus, seating them in the vacant seats. We would have to vacate over six hundred seats. At least that many people saw Jesus after his resurrection, and there were physical contacts made with them. This was not something that was just a figment of their imagination. It was a real contact.

Now, the question is, "Did he really die or were they just meeting somebody whom people thought had died but really hadn't?" To answer that you need to go again to the evidence in history. As surely as his resurrection appearances are infallible proof, the reality of his death is stark and clear. Jesus of Nazareth died on a Roman cross. He was charged by the court to be put to death, and the executioners charged with his death were Roman soldiers who were not known for their tenderness or gentleness. They took a certain delight in the crucifixion process, especially that part where they tested the body to be sure the criminal was dead. When they approached Jesus' limp form on the cross (after he declared, "Father, into Thy hands I commend My spirit"), they discovered he was dead. A Roman spear is stabbed into his side. Blood and water gush out of his side. There's medical evidence, verifiable proof that this man is dead.

Jesus is taken from the cross, carried to a place where his preliminary embalming is done. And then he is placed into a tomb carved out of solid rock. Now, think. You will find some place in mythology the suggestion that there was perhaps a secret exit in that cave where he was buried. But the fact is that the people who buried him were charged not only with his execution, but also with the task of verifying that there was no possible way that the body could be stolen. He is put in a rock tomb. The only access is from the front where a giant stone is rolled. Those stones require the strength of several people to move them. That's the reason the women coming on the first day of the week following the Sabbath to finish the embalming job say to themselves *en route,* "Who will remove the stone for us?" They know that even the group of them will not be able to move it by their own strength. Soldiers are posted there. The seal of imperial Rome has been put on the stone. This stone can't be moved without there being some evidence of it, and whoever would attempt to move it to steal the body would do so at the risk of his own life. With Roman soldiers there, the sealed tomb, the giant stone, the dead body, we're dealing with an infallible proof that he rose from the dead.

The risen Jesus meets a mixed assortment of people in various situations. He meets individuals: Mary Magdalene, Simon Peter, Thomas Didymus. He also addresses ten men in a room who are fugitives running for their lives. That's a story in its own right. He meets with sixty bewildered businessmen at the place where they return to their former business because they cannot compute what's going on in all the mystery and the marvel of the resurrection. This has never happened before. He meets his most vicious persecutor, Saul of Tarsus, who is bent on killing anybody who had anything to do with Jesus because he didn't believe Jesus was Messiah, resurrected Son of God. And when Jesus meets Saul of Tarsus on the road to Damascus, Saul falls before him and recognizes reality.

Then there was the time, probably in Galilee, as he was teaching on the kingdom, that as many as five hundred people were present. There's a body of physical evidence that just *is there;* it is *credible.* The purpose today is not to tally this for the sake of an intellectual accomplishment, but to say that we are dealing with a raw reality, and the only way to elude that reality is by ignorance or bare denial. You may say, "Well, I just choose not to believe this. I don't want to believe it." There's nothing that anyone can do to change the mind of a person who refuses to investigate the evidence. Nor is there anything that can be done for a Christian who determines, "Well, I know Jesus rose from the dead, but I don't feel so good today." Today is not to make us *feel good.* Today is to make us *think straight.* We have started by looking at the credibility of the resurrection, but I primarily want to talk about the *live-ability* of the resurrection. This is the stuff that life is made of. When Jesus says, "Because I live, you shall live also," he's not saying, "Because I live, you'll go to heaven someday," though that is true. That's part of the magnificent arrangement of salvation. He is saying, "Because I live, I can touch you where you live right now."

In the encounters that Jesus has after his resurrection, three specific spiritual-emotional issues are encountered that are common to human experience. The first of these is *grief:* that which hurts and gives the intense feeling of pain. The second is the experience of *struggling with sin* or a weakness or our own sense of inadequacy. The third is the dilemma of *doubt,* or the fear that we don't have the faith that it takes to win in the tough times. These are the questions that come, and they are real and valid questions. And those things, the weeping or the pain, the struggle or the failure or doubt or unbelief are epitomized in three people whom Jesus encounters after his resurrection. In each one of these situations, we see the power of the resurrection to teach a truth, a truth that applies to the most practical details of our lives when we face challenges like that: pain, tears, grief, sorrow. Or when we face struggles: sin, temptation, failure. Or when we face doubt and unbelief.

The first concerns Mary Magdalene, a *weeping* woman. She was weeping at the tomb. She was weeping at the tomb because she presumed the body had been stolen. She was among that group of people who had come to Jesus' burial and entombment, who had later returned to the tomb with the purpose of finishing the embalming task. The women had asked among themselves, "How will we roll the stone back?" They knew the soldiers would be there, but they also knew the soldiers would not be interested in assisting them. "Who will move the stone for us?" But when they arrived the stone was gone, and there was an angelic presence in the place of the soldiers. The women were afraid, except for Mary. As she stood, looking around, she began to weep because it appeared that the body of the Savior had been removed, perhaps as some kind of violation or as some effort at mocking his memory. And as she stood there weeping, she heard a voice. She thought it was the gardener who had come to the garden area to go about his daily duties. But when she turned, she discovered it was Jesus. Recognizing him when he spoke her name, she cried, "Master," and gripped him in an embrace.

I want to take a moment now and stop at that point of embrace, for the most practical of reasons. If someone you have thought dead is alive, someone who had changed your life by their power, you would have run to embrace that person too. That's what had happened in Mary's life. She once was tormented by demonic powers and Jesus had cast seven demons out of her. But it's by reason of that embrace that some of the most incredible constructions have been put around Jesus and Mary's relationship. I want to take a moment with that, because to get the essence of the truth about Mary and what Jesus is saying of her, we need to be rid of some unfortunate fabrications.

Suppose you were to make a list and give it to everybody in the room today and ask people to check the things that are true of Mary Magdalene, and you put on that list, "beautiful woman, young woman, former prostitute, close friend of Jesus, possible girlfriend of Jesus, seductress of Jesus, paramour of Jesus." Some people would just say, "all of the above," because that's the picture you usually get. However, not one of the things on the list can you find anywhere in the historic record. Every one of them has been developed on the strength of the embrace that happened in the garden that day. Yet, any logical person with any sense, seeing somebody who now is alive that was thought to be dead would rejoice and embrace that person.

There's just no evidence that Mary was a prostitute. At least there's no record of it in the Bible. I've heard preachers suggest she had been. But they need to know that's just folklore, not fact. The fact is, where you see Mary mentioned it's usually with the group of women who were a support group to the disciples in their travels. And when you read the list and the description of them, most of them there were mothers, mothers to some of the men in that group. There was Jesus' mother, there's the mother of James and John. Mary Magdalene was probably old enough to be Jesus' mother. The fact that he cast demons out of her does not indicate what her former involvement in sin may have been, nor does it say anything about her age. It's probably evidence that she's a mature, seasoned, experienced woman who's not too easily spooked by circumstances that she remains standing there at the empty tomb when the rest of the women ran because of their fear. Something weird has happened here. She stays there and weeps because she feels the weight of the moment. Mary Magdalene's embrace of Jesus is the embrace of someone who's been greatly affected by the power of God and is very happy to see that her Savior is alive.

It is in what Jesus says at that moment that we learn a tremendous truth. He said to her after the embrace, "No, don't cling to me anymore." Let me take the freedom to play with this for a moment in order to make my point clearly. When Jesus said, "Don't cling to me anymore," some people want to extrapolate, to infer that he meant, "Don't...I just...we've got to stop meeting this way." Or that Jesus was saying, "Don't do that. I just can't stand it when you do that. I only have so much strength. I'm only human." That's what they think he was implying. Or, "You have to let go. No touchie the holy bod'." But that's not at all what this is all about. Instead, Jesus is saying, "You mustn't continue clinging to me anymore." For Mary, the embrace may have been a spontaneous response to the pain she had endured at losing the Master, but he had to let her know that she could no longer "keep down" the triumphant Lord. His words are words of comfort to her, but he must leave her nonetheless: not to the grave, but to glory, as he ascends to the Father. What he's saying is, "I have come, risen from the dead not only that you might be comforted in your pain, but that you might know that there is conquest over your pain."

I have been preaching recently about how Christians deal with pain. Even in churches today there is this notion that we overcome by going through interminable processes of human engineering and programs in order to finally surmount the history of our past. What Jesus said was, "I have risen from the dead, and I do care about your past and the pain that is involved and the tears you experienced. I care, whether it's the grieving for a person that you just recently lost who was very dear to you, or if it was some terrible tragedy and ache that comes out of your personal experience, recent or distant. But the message," Jesus says, "is that I have come to *transform* your moment, not simply to talk about it."

Dear ones, the gospel of Jesus Christ comes by the

power of the resurrection and is just that dramatic. The Lord severs the power of sin and pain to hold you in your past, and he comes to deliver you completely by his resurrection presence. He is telling you, "I will not only comfort you, I will bring my conquering power to bear into your life. I am ascending to God, to your God." And the message is, don't cling to things that are temporal solutions. Reach out to the hand of God that is reaching to you with power to touch you, with the confidence that resurrection *liveability* has to do with the pain and the hurt you have. Reach to the Lord with it. Whether you've walked with Christ a hundred years or whether for the first time you today are opening your mind to understanding that you need to come and walk with him, reach out to him and say, "Lord, I would receive your conquest over the matters of past grief and sorrow."

When Mary was there on that occasion by the tomb with Jesus, the words were given to her with direction, "Now, go tell the disciples," and specifically Jesus said, "and Peter." Go tell Peter too. Not because he wasn't a disciple, but because Peter, Simon Peter had a particular problem right at that moment. Peter is a remarkable person in the Scriptures. He's outstanding for a combination of reasons, but the most notable one is the incredible leadership qualities that are present with him. He's a dynamic man, a strong man. There's nothing wimpy about this guy. When I call him a struggling man today, it's not because he's a weak man. He's a man who had encountered the limits of his strength, and was coming to terms with his need of something beyond himself. It wasn't that Peter didn't already know the Lord in some respect, but he was discovering something this day that was in another dimension. Perhaps there are people here today who have walked with Christ for some time, and you need another dimension of discovering what he is like. Or perhaps there is some guy here like Peter. You're a strong man, but down deep inside, you know you're not as strong as it seems, even though you've given it your best. You stumble and fail at times. Even though no one else may know about it, you know. Peter first met Jesus when he was a fisherman up in Galilee. He wasn't the modern American kind of fisherman. You've seen those guys lolling in a boat on a summer afternoon with their pole up there, waiting for a nibble while their eyes were covered by a straw hat, dozing in the back of the boat. I'm talking about a real redneck fisherman. I'm talking about a guy for hours at a time struggling with large nets. We're talking commercial fishing. Peter is a tough guy. He's the kind of guy who, if he can't get a netful of fish by pulling the net in, he'll try and swear them in. He's a man's man in every sense of the word.

He had been following Jesus now for some time, and the night before Jesus was crucified, Peter was with them when Jesus said, "All of you will forsake me." Those disciples didn't know exactly what Jesus was talking about; all they knew was a sense of foreboding about the next day. And Peter stood among the others and leveled his gaze at Jesus. "Lord, if everybody else forsakes you, I never will." And Jesus looked back gently at him, and he said, "Peter, before the rooster crows announcing tomorrow morning's sunrise, you will deny three times." Peter didn't believe that, but it happened. And we remember that it happened. But don't forget that Peter did make an effort to carry out his promise. When Jesus was out there on the Mount of Olives and the Garden of Gethsemane and the crowd came to capture him led by Judas the traitor, Peter was the first one to rise, pull out a sword, and go right into the crowd. I'm talking swinging! And a man dodging to get out of his way had his ear clipped. Jesus stopped Peter, reached out, touched the man's ear, and healed it. He told Peter, "Put your sword away. That's not going to win today." Peter was bewildered by that, but he had said only hours before, "If everybody else forsakes you," and already the disciples are beginning to disappear. This is a tough moment. They're not cowards, but they don't understand everything that's happening.

Now Peter follows the crowd that is taking Jesus to the place of his trial. He and John are the only two who remain. Don't forget that. We say, "Peter's denial! Peter denied the Lord!" Peter is a strong man who's doing the best he can, and he has tried to defend Jesus. Now he's going to stick with him, and he gets just inside the door of the high priest's house with the trial about to begin, and a little girl standing there says, "I've seen you with this man. You're . . . you're one of these Jesus people." Peter says, "No, I'm not." I have an opinion about that first denial. I don't think it's the denial of a coward. I think Peter has pressed this far because he doesn't want to fail. It's a man trying to do his best. He's there thinking, "You know, if there's any way I can get him out of here, I will do it. I want to study the situation, and I don't want to give away who I really am right now." Later, the second and third time he denies the Lord, each situation is different. Finally, he is warming his hands with a group of men around the fire, and one of them says, "I know that you're one of those Galileans who travel with Jesus." Peter swears and says, "No, I'm not!" He is afraid now. Then the rooster crows and the morning is about to dawn, and Peter hears the sound and remembers what Jesus had said. The Bible says that he went out from that place, down the quiet streets of Jerusalem. He walked to some location, we know not where, and the Scripture says, "Peter wept bitterly."

When Jesus says to Mary, "Go find my disciples and Peter," he is aware that there is a man who feels so deeply his failure that he doubts that he will ever find a way back. He has compromised himself and violated his word.

Hear me, please, this morning. Whoever you are, it is not just weeping women, because men weep, too, and have pain and tears. And it is not just men who struggle, because women have struggles and failures as well. The gender isn't the point; the human experience is. There's not only a credibility to the resurrection, there's a *live-ability*. Jesus' appearance to these two people proves that. The Bible records that later that day of his resurrection, Jesus went specifically and personally to find Peter to tell him, "Peter, I'm alive. You are forgiven. Peter, the resurrection means there is forgiveness for your failure. I know the struggle, and you tried and you are forgiven." There are people on every point of the spectrum here today in terms of spiritual experience to whom on this Easter morning the Lord wants to say all over again: "I am alive, and you are forgiven. I understand your pain, but stop embracing the temporal. Reach to the rule of God to enter your pain."

There's a *third* person I want to mention in this message. His name is Thomas, Thomas Didymus. Mary Magdalene, Simon Peter, Thomas Didymus. Didymus isn't really a last name. It means that he was a twin. Thomas is called Doubting Thomas to this day, but he is not just a *doubter,* he is a tightfisted *realist.* He is hard-nosed.

On one occasion, Jesus was talking to the disciples. "We're going to go over to..." and he names a place where they are going. Everyone in the group knows that if you go there, you'll be in dangerous territory, especially with Jesus' reputation as a healer, an evangelist whom the authorities dislike. Jesus says, "We're going anyway." The others had warned, "We can't go there. It's dangerous." But Jesus is resolute, "We're going." So Thomas turns to the rest of the group (I just love this) and says, "Come on, let's go and die with him." Cheery O'Leery. The guy is a bundle of fun.

On another occasion we are allowed to see a different facet of Thomas's penetrating insistence on realism. Jesus said, "Let not your heart be troubled; you believe in God, believe also in Me. In My Father's house are many mansions; if it were not so, I would have told you" (John 14:1–2 NKJV). He is talking about Heaven. He said, "I go to prepare a place for you, and if I go and prepare a place for you, I'll come again and receive you to myself. Where I'm going you know and the way you know." And Thomas drew him up, "Wait. Wait. Wait. Wait." It's as though Thomas was saying, "I was with you to a certain point. I understand. You are talking about heaven and all that. But when you said, 'Where I'm going, you know the way.' No, I don't. And if we're talking about heaven, I want to know it right now. Lord, I don't know where you're going. You tell me right now. I want to get this straight." So many people would say,

"Well, Lord, I know that you'll take care of it and help me understand it in time." But not Thomas. He says, "Let's don't go any further right now. Let's get this straight before we take another step. Where?" He wanted it cleared up right then and there: nothing fuzzy.

Thomas was not present that Easter evening when ten of the disciples were hiding for fear of the authorities. Now, their fear of the authorities was justified, because the word was out that the tomb was empty, and they were looking for anybody they could blame, and it might cost them their lives. They were in rooms that were probably barred and shuttered. They were probably in the same place they'd met with Jesus the night before his crucifixion, in the upper room. And as they were gathered there, the Bible says Jesus, unlimited by time and space, not a ghost, but unrestricted by time and space, entered the room while everything was locked. He just entered. As he stood there, they understandably thought he was a ghost. After all, things don't just come into rooms that way. And Jesus said, "Come on, just touch me. I'm not a ghost." Then he sat down and he ate a meal with them. This happened a number of times in the post-resurrection appearances. We are not dealing with something spooky. We are dealing with something transcendent and someone who has come to master all things. He is the Lord of creation.

Thomas wasn't there when that happened that night. Who knows where he was? But he heard the report from the guys the next week, and he said very pointedly, "Wait a minute. I know what happened at the cross. His side was ripped open, and his hands were stabbed through." And here are his words, "Except I put my hand in his side, except my fingers touch where the nails went through his hands, I will not believe."

It is a week later. The disciples are gathered in the same place again. It is there that Jesus appears a second time to that group. Thomas is present this time. Jesus, coming into the room, moves directly to Thomas. "Reach forth your hand," Jesus says. "Put your hand right there. Here, touch my hands and be not faithless but believing." The hard-nosed realist has met the ultimate pragmatist, because Jesus is very practical.

Oh, I weary of the fact that on any given Easter any preacher or teacher in a given church is going to face a certain number of people whom I understand very well. I hold no criticism toward you for this, but there has come into your mind the notion that everything to do with Jesus and God and the Bible is some kind of an ethereal, mystical, poetic sort of impractical, purely otherworldly message. Sometimes you need that. But what we really need today is a practical word from God, and Jesus says to Thomas, who is just about as pragmatic as you get, "I want to tell you: here, just touch right here." Dear friend, the hand of God reaches to us in the most practical details of our life, and the Lord says, "I want you to know, I know the things you have questions about and doubts about, and I will address them directly if you will ask me to."

His name was Phil, and the service was over. He came down to the front of the sanctuary as I was sitting there talking with someone. He said, "Can I just have a word with you?"

I said, "Sure. What's your name?" Phil was about twenty-six or twenty-seven years old.

He said, "Sir, I've come to this place, and I've never been here before. I'd like to know God, but I don't know how to know him." He went on, "I don't really believe."

I said, "Well, Phil, that's okay. Let me tell you what to do. Will you pray a prayer?"

"Well, I don't know if I can because I don't believe."

I replied, "Well, that's okay. You'll hear what the prayer is. I'll tell you." And I told him in advance.

He said, "Yeah, I'll pray that."

Here's what the prayer was: "God, I don't even know if you're there, but I do ask you this sincerely from my heart: If you will manifest yourself to me, then I will serve you with all my heart." And we said "Amen." He said to me, "Thank you." And he left.

That same evening, he went down the street some miles from here, walked into a restaurant, and sat down and placed his order. He was sitting at the counter as someone came up and sat down behind him. They began to talk. Then he saw the person had a Bible, and he asked, "What do you think about that?" The person said, "Well, I'd be glad to talk any way you would like." The newcomer began to talk to him about Jesus. Phil said, "You know, that's a strange thing that you'd come and sit by me and you've got a Bible. Just a few minutes ago I prayed a prayer. I asked that if God was real that he would somehow show himself to me, and I gotta tell you that this makes me kind of nervous on the possibility that that's what you're doing here."

Phil came to Christ in those next two or three days. He was honest with God. In a church in Alliance, Ohio, this very Easter morning the message is being preached by the pastor who has served two churches as senior pastor for the last fifteen years. His name is Philip Shepard, and he knows the life of Jesus Christ and transmits it to other people. But it started with a guy saying, "Hey, God, I don't even know that you're real."

The Lord will reach to you the same way he reached to Thomas and to Phil Shepard. There was a little boy whose name was Gregory. Gregory and his mom and dad and his two sisters are a part of our congregation here. He's six years old now. The story I'm telling begins almost two years ago when Gregory was four. You need to know this about Gregory: He was born three months premature. He was a twin. Andrew, his brother in the womb, died at birth. Gregory survived. He wasn't expected to, and was given only a 5 percent chance of living. "If this baby survives," the doctors said, "he'll be a vegetable." He survived, and as you will shortly discover, he transcended anything that medical hopes had projected. Gregory's present condition is similar to a mild case of cerebral palsy, but it's not as seriously impacting.

It was about two years ago that Gregory said to his father, "Dad, where's heaven?"

His dad, who is a doctor, said, "Well, Gregory, you know, it's up there. It's up above."

Gregory said, "Way above? Up in the sky?"

His dad said, "Nobody knows how high." (Theologians can't even answer these questions; talking to a four-year-old, what do you say?)

As the conversation proceeded it was clear that the reason for Gregory's curiosity was that he knows that was where his brother Andrew was, and he thought about

Andrew sometimes. He wanted to know Andrew's condition and maybe where Andrew was. About four months went by from that conversation, and the family was going on a holiday to the Hawaiian Islands. It was Thanksgiving time, and they'd just gotten on the plane and were taking off from LAX. Gregory was sitting there by the window, staring out, and when the plane started up, just after it had been airborne, he turned to his dad and said, "Dad, where are we now?"

Dad looked out the window and said, "We're over Santa Monica Bay, son."

"Well, how high are we?"

"About five thousand feet."

"Is this way up?"

Still not cognizant of what was on Gregory's mental agenda, he replied, "No, we're going to go a lot higher than this, probably about 35,000 feet."

The little boy's eyes went back out the window, and the plane shot through an extended fog bank. He was just riveted, looking out there, not knowing what to expect. Then they rose beyond the clouds and broke into the sunlight. He looked up and asked, "Dad, where are we now?"

"Well, son, we're up above the clouds."

He looked out again, and looked back to his father and said, "Dad, where's heaven?"

The boy's father suddenly realized that his little son had expected that above the clouds maybe he'd see Andrew and maybe he'd see heaven. He talked and explained to him and helped the little guy get a better understanding. From his father's explanation Gregory captured a sense that heaven is something more than what he had a notion of. Nearly a full year went by and almost nothing was said on the subject until just last Christmas time. Gregory, now five years of age, playing around the house one day, came over to his dad and blurted out, "Dad, how do you get to heaven?"

His dad asked, "Well, son, how do you think?"

Greg said, "Well, it's not by plane."

The man laughed and he said, "That's right, son."

Greg continued on, "It's not by boat."

"That's right too."

He said, "It's not by car. It's not by train."

His dad could recognize that he had made a whole list of things.

Gregory said, "It is not by walking. It is not by bus. Dad, I know how you get to heaven."

"How's that, Greg?"

"By hand."

Puzzled, his dad asked, "By hand?"

And Gregory said, "Dad, the only way anybody can get to heaven is by the hand of God."

That story speaks so profoundly to me when I see Jesus reaching out to his friends, to Simon Peter with forgiveness, to Mary with peace over grief, to Thomas the hardnosed, saying, "Look at my hands and don't be faithless but believing."

This morning I doubt that there is one of us who in some way or another doesn't need to reach out and take the hand of the Lord this Easter morning. We need to say, "Jesus, resurrected King, I receive what you have for me." There are grieving hearts that need to recognize that

Christ will not only comfort, he will bring conquest over the pain of the past or the immediate struggle of a failure or the doubts that obstruct. And there are, along with the host of us who have begun our life in Christ, precious people who are here this morning who have never begun life with Jesus. Whatever the need in your life, won't you take the hand of the Risen One?

THANKSGIVING

8
Gratitude

Jack Graham
1 Thessalonians 5:18

In every thing give thanks: for this is the will of God in Christ Jesus concerning you.

*T*hink with me first about the *attitude of gratitude,* because in giving thanks we are to continually give thanks unto God. This is God's will for every Christian. When we translate *thanksgiving* into *thanksliving* we give thanks in all times, in all seasons, for all things. The psalmist said, "I will bless the Lord at all times." That means good days as well as bad days.

Bad days do come. As a matter of fact, you know you're having a bad day when you call your answering service and they tell you it's none of your business. You also know it's going to be a bad day when you're in a traffic jam, your horn gets stuck and won't stop honking, and you're behind a group of Hell's Angels. That is a bad day! You also know it's going to be a bad day when you sink your teeth into a big juicy steak and your teeth stay there. You know that's going to be a bad day.

But we ought to be able to give thanks because for the believer thanksgiving is the first response. You recall the story of the ten lepers in the Gospel of Luke. Those ten men with a loathsome disease, a deadly disease, were cured by the Lord Jesus Christ. They went away rejoicing, but only one of those ten returned to say "thanks." I'm certain that all of them were thankful, all of them were grateful, but only one returned and fell on his face and said, "Thank you, Lord, for saving me and delivering me." It is by the grace of God and the goodness of God that we are able to say "thanks."

As a matter of fact our English root for the word *gratitude* is the same as the word *grace*. Grace and gratitude are twin sisters. Don't get so busy, don't get so hurried that you don't pause to praise. Also in our English language the words *think* and *thank* have the same root. So when we think, when we stop, when we reflect on the grace of God in our life we automatically say, "Thank you." How many times blessings just bypass us day by day because we don't think! But how grateful we are for the gift of eternal life through Jesus Christ our Lord. Our lives, therefore, should be lived as children of God saying, "Thank you."

The other day I took our seven-year-old, Josh, to the toy store. We went to buy a special toy that he had been wanting. When we arrived at the store we picked out what he wanted. It was a good time for the two of us. We paid the money and went out. When your kids grow up, they learn to mature and they learn to do the things that you hope they'll do automatically. As soon as we walked out the door into the parking lot he turned and put his arms around me and said, "Daddy, thank you." I was so excited that I nearly took him back into the store to buy him another toy. It's just wonderful when you see your children respond in that manner. Don't you think God the Father desires for us to return our thanks unto him in daily ways for daily blessings?

I heard about an old lady who bowed her head and said, "Thank you, Lord, for these vittles." Someone overheard and asked, "Lady, what are vittles?" She answered, "These are the blessings God gives me, my food to eat." That person responded, "Don't you know you are going to have that food to eat whether you thank God for it or not?" Her answer was very instructive: "Well, perhaps so, but everything tastes better when I'm thankful." In life everything goes better, everything tastes better when we are thankful.

Psychologists tell us that gratitude, thanksgiving, is the healthiest of all human emotions. Hans Selye, who is considered the father of stress studies, has said that gratitude produces more positive emotional energy than any other attitude in life. Gratitude is the antidote for all negative emotions and negative experiences in our lives, whether they be bitterness or fear or anxiety or discouragement or depression. In everything give thanks because thanksgiving positively counteracts and challenges the damaging and destructive emotions in the stressful lives we live.

It has been well said that a thankful heart enjoys the blessing twice—when it receives the blessing and when it remembers the blessing. When you have blessings and you are thankful continually for those blessings, you can just remember them and enjoy them again and again and again. This is the attitude of gratitude—in everything give thanks.

Now there are some *gratitude busters.* I would mention several here. One attitude that will destroy this gratitude attitude is *conceit*—the attitude of pride. It is the attitude that says, "I deserve what I have, I earn what I have!" Remember this—pride comes before a fall. I might add that pride also comes before a great deal of disappointment. Pride will destroy thanksgiving and the attitude of gratitude in your life.

Something else that will destroy gratitude is a *critical spirit,* what we might call pettiness. Constantly complaining will rob us of our joy. Thanksgiving, the attitude of gratitude, is a habit; it is a good habit. A critical spirit is a habit too. A critical spirit always finds fault. Someone who is constantly critical is never satisfied, never content. Rather than being *humbly grateful* this person is *grumbly hateful.* Many people live like that; they are just never happy, never satisfied. There's always a reason to give thanks. And by the way, don't grumble because you don't have what you want, but be thankful that you didn't get what you deserve.

Conceit will kill this attitude; a *critical spirit* will destroy it, and so will *carelessness.* So often we get accustomed to our blessings, don't we? We get used to them. If the stars came out only once a year, we would stay out all night just to look at them. And we often take for granted the blessings of life, even some of the wonderful blessings.

The children of Israel were in the desert, stranded before they got to the promised land, and yet God promised to provide for them. And God did provide for them in a miraculous way. He sent manna from heaven to sustain them, to strengthen them. Every morning they got up there was this fresh bread from God lying on the ground; all they had to do was to collect and eat. When they first received the miracle they were so excited about the miracle. They were so blessed by the manna. But as time wore on they grew tired of the manna. You know, a little boy got up in the morning for twenty years and said, "What are we having for breakfast, Mom?"

And she said, "Manna."

"What are we having for lunch?"

She said, "Manna."

"What are we having for dinner?"

The answer, "Manna." Like the old song, "Manna in the morning, manna in the evening, manna at the supper time." They had manna all the time. Finally these people said "Ugh, we hate, we loathe this bread." They had a miracle every day, but they got used to their miracle, and they were no longer satisfied.

Give thanks with a grateful heart. That's the attitude of gratitude. In everything give thanks.

I want you to think with me, second, about the *altitude of gratitude*. You've heard that old statement, "It's not your aptitude, but your attitude that determines your altitude." Let me add that it's your gratitude that determines your altitude.

Gratitude will absolutely change our lives. It will alter our perspective in life. I heard about a college co-ed who wrote her parents the following letter.

Dear Mom and Dad,

I'm sorry I've been so long in writing. Unfortunately all my stationery was destroyed the night our dorm was set on fire by demonstrators. I'm out of the hospital now and the doctors say my eyesight should return sooner or later. The wonderful boy, Bill, who rescued me from the fire kindly offered to share his apartment with me until my dorm room is rebuilt. He comes from a grand family, so you won't be surprised when I tell you we're going to be married in a short while. In fact, since you've always wanted a grandchild, you'll be glad to know you'll be grandparents next month.

P.S. Please disregard the above practice in English composition. There was no fire. I haven't been to the hospital. I'm not pregnant, and I don't even have a boyfriend. But I did get a "D" in French and an "F" in chemistry. I just wanted to be sure you received the news in perspective.

Gratitude will change your perspective. You can grovel and gripe, or you can glory in the presence of God with praise and thanksgiving. After all, in heaven we're going to spend eternity praising and thanking God. We ought to start practicing now.

Praise and thanksgiving will lift you into the heavenlies. If you feel life is closing in on you, if you feel like every door is shut, if you feel airtight in a compartment and you can't get out, then praise God!

Thanksgiving enlarges our lives. Do you know why? The

more I am thankful the larger will be the range of my blessings. If I limit my gratitude, then my life will be narrow and my perspective will be limited. If I build fences around my little blessing, my life will be very small. My life will be very selfish. Thanksgiving, the altitude of it, enables me to lift and look beyond myself.

Read the Psalms. There you will see praise and thanksgiving continually. He's thanking God for things on the earth. He's thanking God for material blessings. He's thanking God for spiritual blessings. He's thanking God for joy. He's thanking God for sorrow. The whole range of human experience is open to us when we give thanks. I have noticed that those whom I have considered to be spiritual giants, those men and women who are taking the world for Jesus Christ, have grateful and gracious hearts. God has lifted them and enlarged them and strengthened them in it. Perhaps this is what Annie Johnson Flint meant when she wrote, "As we offer our small rejoicing for the love that surrounds our days. All the wonderful works of the goodness of God open before our gaze. And through the gates of our narrow thanksgiving we shall enter the courts of praise."

It is by praise and thanksgiving that our capacity to receive God's blessing is enriched and enlarged. So is our comprehension to receive greater blessings. Too many of us are constantly adding to our prayer list, but we ought to be adding to our praise list.

I know it is not always easy to praise God. It's not always easy when you're stuck in traffic, thirty minutes late to work, to praise God and thank God. It isn't easy when the doctor's report is not what you'd prayed for, not what you'd hoped for. It isn't easy to praise God when someone you love walks out on you. There are many times in life when it is almost humanly impossible to praise God. But remember this, God will never ask you to do anything he will not enable you to do. If it is the will of God for you to give thanks (and it is, according to 1 Thess. 5:18), he will strengthen you to do it. To give thanks in everything, in the midst of everything, even in your midnight hour, is possible for God's people. You see, thanksgiving will not always change my circumstances, but thanksgiving will change what my circumstances do to me. That is the altitude of gratitude. It changes my perspective. Praise and thanksgiving get me off the ground and into the glories where I can see with a new perspective even sometimes through tears with thanksgiving. I can see a sovereign God who loves me, who has a perfect purpose for my life, who is in all and over all and above all. That is the altitude of gratitude.

There is a third concern that this text raises. I want you to think with me for a few moments about the *latitude of gratitude*.

By latitude, I mean the width of it. Do you remember the Philippian jailer who came to Christ in Acts 16? How did that jailer come to know Christ as Savior? We say, "Well, because of the earthquake. It scared him to death." No, it wasn't the earthquake. The earthquake caused him to want to commit suicide. Why did that jailer come to Christ along with his whole family, eventually? Well, there were two men in that prison, Paul and Silas. At the midnight hour they were praising God. They were singing hymns of praise and thanksgiving to God. When the earthquake came and they were released from their bonds along with all the other prisoners, they were able by the testimony of their thanksgiving to lead that Philippian jailer to Christ. Why? Because thanksgiving is a testimony that extends the love of God to others.

When we realize how blessed we are, we will want to be a blessing to someone else. We want to share our blessings. It's far better to be a blessing than even to receive a blessing. Jesus said, "It is more blessed to give than to receive" (Acts 20:35 NIV). The latitude of gratitude is the joy of expressing our thanks—to extend the grace of God and the goodness of God to others. The moment you receive a blessing it's only natural to say "thank you" and then to share with someone else.

How do we share the grace of God? In our church we celebrate Thanksgiving with an event we call "To Dallas with Love." Our members feed over 5,000 people, helping them also with clothing and other needs. But we never stop there. We share the gospel. At our last celebration a young African-American came to Christ. We also gave him some clothes, gave him a new suit. He shared the meal with us and afterward said, "You folks have just done everything for me. You've given me Jesus; you've given me a brand-new suit. You've given me a meal. Now, what can I do? Can I stay around and help clean up? Can I do something to return with thanksgiving what God has done for me?" That's the latitude of gratitude. As soon as you receive the blessing you want to turn around and share with someone else. How do we share this latitude?

First, by *singing*. Psalm 28:7 says, "The LORD is my strength and my shield; my heart trusted in him, and I am helped: therefore my heart greatly rejoiceth; and with my song will I praise him." We praise God with the testimony song. All of the Psalms are psalms of praise and thanksgiving to God. "Forget not all his benefits," the psalmist tells us. By singing we share the latitude of gratitude.

Then, by *sharing* we give the latitude of gratitude. By giving to others. We are to give not grudgingly but with thanksgiving. It's a privilege to give to my church. I don't count it something I *have* to do. It is something I'm *privileged* to do, to participate in the ministry of the church. To forget about ourselves and to live for others rather than living for ourselves—that is the breadth and width and height of gratitude.

Another way to share the latitude of gratitude is by *soul winning.* The greatest cause of thanksgiving in my life is the day I accepted Christ as my Savior. I will be forever grateful for the indescribable gift, the unspeakable gift of Jesus, for eternal life in him. But the next greatest experience in my life is anytime I have the privilege of telling someone else about Jesus. If you're having problems with the latitude of gratitude in your life, you might ask yourself, "How long has it been since I've shared my faith with someone else?" If you'll share your faith with someone else and especially if you have the joy of leading that someone to know faith in Christ, your heart will overflow with thanksgiving to God. You will be overwhelmed by joy. Life's possibilities unfold before us when we are grateful. What a wonderful time this is to give thanks by sharing a testimony of faith in Jesus Christ!

May we rejoice on this day of Thanksgiving. For in doing so, our attitude, our altitude, and our latitude will reflect a grateful heart.

9

The Attitude
of Gratitude

James Merritt

R *1 Thessalonians 5:18*
udyard Kipling was a great British poet whose writings have blessed many of us, including a generation gone by. Rudyard Kipling was a very famous writer even before he died, and made a great deal of money at his trade.

A newspaper reporter came up to him once and said, "Mr. Kipling, I just read that somebody calculated that the money you make from your writings amounts to over one hundred dollars a word." Mr. Kipling raised his eyebrows and said, "Really, I certainly wasn't aware of that." The reporter cynically reached into his pocket and pulled out a one hundred dollar bill and gave it to Kipling and said, "Here's a one hundred dollar bill, Mr. Kipling. Now you give me one of your one-hundred-dollar words."

Rudyard Kipling looked at that piece of currency for a moment, took it and folded it up and put it in his pocket and said, "Thanks."

Well, the word *thanks* is certainly a one-hundred-dollar word. In fact, I would say it is more like a million-dollar word. That is one word that is too *seldom heard,* too *rarely spoken,* and too *often forgotten.*

If any nation *ought* to be thankful to God and grateful for his goodness, it ought to be America. If any people in America ought to be thankful to God and grateful for his goodness, it ought to be Christians. If any group of Christians ought to be thankful to God and grateful for his goodness, it ought to be the Christians in this fellowship. We ought to have an attitude of gratitude.

In this wonderful profound verse of Scripture Paul gives us three principles concerning this attitude of gratitude that every child of God *ought* to have.

First, I want you to see that *gratitude is always to be expressed.*

We are commanded to "Give thanks." Now, that is excellent advice because a grateful person will be a happier person; a grateful person will be a healthier person; a grateful person will be a holier person.

But this is more than just good advice. It is a command. Gratitude is not an option. You are just as obligated to give God your thanks as you are to give God your tithe. It is a sin to be ungrateful. As a matter of fact, there may be no greater sin on the face of the earth than the sin of ingratitude.

Shakespeare described ingratitude as a "Marble-Hearted Fiend." That is, he said that an ingrate had the heart of solid marble.

Shakespeare went on to say, "I hate ingratitude more in man than lying, vainness, babbling, drunkenness, or any taint of vice, whose strong corruption inhabits our frail blood." Shakespeare said again, "How sharper than a serpent's tooth it is to have a thankless child." I know of nothing that stings the heart of a parent as a child who is ungrateful for what the parent does for him.

The blind poet Milton said this: "He that is ungrateful has no guilt but one; all other crimes may pass for virtues in him." That is, he said every other fault in a person is a virtue compared to the vice of ingratitude.

Someone else has written these words: "The thief may have some streaks of honesty in him, the deadbeat spots of honor, the liar hours when he loves the truth, the libertine occasions when he has impulses to be pure; but there is nothing redemptive in the ingrate."

Also, listen to this blistering indictment of the ungrateful soul. "Trust the ungrateful soul with money—and he will steal it; with honor—and he will betray it; with virtue—and he will violate it; with love—and, with hellish alchemy, he will transmute it into lust; with your good name—and he will besmirch it."

Ingratitude is the mark of rank worldliness. It is the mark of an unbeliever. It is the character of an infidel to be ungrateful. Paul, in describing a lost world, said in Romans 1:21, "Because, although they knew God, they did not glorify Him as God, nor were thankful" (NKJV). You are never more like a lost man, an unbeliever, than when you are ungrateful.

That is why I say that gratitude is always to be expressed. We are to give thanks. Have you ever thanked that person who led you to Jesus Christ? Have you ever thanked that Sunday school teacher who so faithfully taught you the Word of God as a child? Have you ever thanked your mother and father for loving you and giving you a good home? Have you ever thanked your wife for being the good mother and homemaker and cook that she is? Have you ever thanked your husband for providing for your material needs and working hard to provide a house to live in and food to eat and clothes to wear?

It is better to say "Thank you" and not mean it than to mean it and not say it. Gratitude is always to be expressed.

Second, *gratitude is always to be expansive.*

We are told to give thanks in "every thing." Those two words make this verse so very difficult. If we were told to thank God in "most things" we could live with it. If we were told to thank God in "good things" we would find the verse a lot easier to accept and obey. But Paul says we are to thank God in "every thing."

Now a caution here is in order. Nowhere in the word of God are we commanded to "feel grateful." Feelings come and feelings go. Feelings can be affected by the weather, by the temperature, by the function of your liver, by how much rest you got the night before. Thanksgiving has nothing to do with feelings. We are not commanded to "feel grateful." It doesn't matter whether things are good or whether things are bad, we are to be grateful.

Now lest you are thinking, "Well, that may be easy for Paul to say," let me tell you that it was *not* easy for Paul to say. Paul had been run out of Thessalonica at the threat of losing his life. He had been beaten, whipped, imprisoned, shipwrecked, stoned, and left for dead. Yet he said, "In every thing give thanks."

In Acts 16 we are told the story of how Paul and Silas were beaten with rods and then whipped and scourged and then thrown into a Philippian prison. But rather than sighing they began singing. I don't know what songs they sang, but I know they were songs of thanksgiving.

Yes, we are indeed to thank God for everything. I believe this "everything" would cover at least three things that would come to us in everyday living: In its expansiveness, we are to be grateful for the *blessings of life*.

Proverbs 10:22 says, "The blessing of the LORD makes one rich, / and He adds no sorrow with it" (NKJV). According to this verse, if you are a Christian you have been blessed by God and if you've been blessed by God you are rich. I like one definition of a Christian that I read not long ago that said, "A Christian is someone who does not have to consult his bankbook to see how wealthy he really is."

Do you thank God for the blessings of life, just the simple, everyday blessings? For example, do you thank God for your daily bread? Did you know that two-thirds of the world go to bed hungry every night? One-third of the world is underfed, and one-third of the world is starving. In fact, thirty people starve to death every minute, and we complain about dirty dishes. Now no one likes dirty dishes, least of all this pastor. But I believe we ought to thank God for dirty dishes. After all, by the stack of evidence in the kitchen every night, I'd say we've all been blessed by God.

It is an unbelievable thing to me to see people who sit down to a meal in a restaurant and begin eating like pigs and dogs, never thanking God for their food. Do you realize your daily bread comes from the hand of your heavenly Father? You should never sit down to a meal without bowing your head and humbly thanking God for the food he has provided for you.

We all ought to have the attitude of that little girl whose father was a disc jockey, a radio announcer. She was invited to a friend's house for dinner. When she arrived the mother asked the little girl if she would honor them by saying the blessing.

It delighted the little girl. She cleared her throat, looked at her wristwatch, and said, "This food, friends, is coming to you through the courtesy of Almighty God." Well, she was right, all food that we eat comes through the courtesy of Almighty God.

We thank God for food, but do you ever thank God for water? Did you know that only 3 percent of the water in this world is fit to drink? Or that only one-third of 1 percent of the world's water is available to drink, and most of that clean water is right here in the United States of America? Over one-half of the world has no access to pure drinking water. Oh, how grateful we ought to be for the blessings of God, especially the small blessings. "Be grateful for venetian blinds. If it weren't for them, it would be curtains for all of us."

In fact, I believe that God's greatest blessings are often found in the smallest things. I heard about an elderly lady who got up in a testimony meeting and said, "There's always something to be thankful for. I only have two teeth, but thank God they both meet."

We ought also to be grateful for the *burdens of life*.

We are told "In everything we are to give thanks." Notice it is *in* everything, not necessarily *for* everything. We are not to be thankful for trouble, but we are to be thankful in the midst of trouble. Indeed, one of the purposes of the trials, troubles, and tribulations that come to us in life is to move us to thanksgiving. Second Corinthians 4:15 says, "For all things are for your sakes, that grace, having spread through the many, may cause thanksgiving to abound to the glory of God" (NKJV).

Everything that happens *to* you also happens *for* you. That is why you are to always give thanks in every situation. Regardless of how bad it may seem to you, God wants to use it in your life to move you to thanksgiving.

Matthew Henry, the famous Bible teacher, was once accosted by thieves and robbed of all of his money. He wrote these words in his diary: "I am so very thankful. First, because I was never robbed before. Second, because although they took my purse they did not take my life. Third, because although they took everything I had, it wasn't very much. Fourth, it was I who was robbed, not I who robbed."

Do you thank him in the bad times as well as in the good? Do you thank him in the midst of trouble as you do in the midst of triumph?

We ought also to be grateful for the *benefits of life.*

Psalm 103:2 says, "Bless the LORD, O my soul, / And forget not all His benefits" (NKJV). Do you ever thank God for just the benefits of being one of his children and one of his creatures? Just for the benefit of living on God's green earth? Aren't you glad that you don't have to pay taxes on sunlight?

If you ever go over to England you will discover that many of the English houses of the eighteenth century are very small in size, and few of them have windows. The reason for this was because of the "window tax," one of the most senseless taxes ever levied by a ruling power. The government was charging houses for the use of the sun when they had more than six windows in the house. When I think about the cost of electricity I shudder to think what would happen if God were to start charging for sunlight.

Aren't you grateful that the air we breathe is free; that we don't have to pay an admission to see a sunset or to hear a bird sing or to smell a rose? What on earth would we do if God, all of a sudden, went on strike and wiped out all of these benefits?

Have you ever thanked God for the benefits of just living in America? You know, so often we gripe about going to work, fighting the traffic, having to put up with a nasty boss, having to pay taxes. Well, the next time you gripe about America and work and paying taxes, think about this: In Russia, a man has to work one hour to earn a loaf of bread. In America he works only six minutes. For a quart of milk the average Russian works one hour and eleven minutes; an American works nine minutes. For a suit of clothes the Russian must work 583 hours; the American works 38 hours. For a plain cotton dress the Russian works 225 hours; an American works four hours.

Oh, don't you forget the benefits of God. We ought to give God thanks in all things. We ought to give God thanks always. Paul reminds us in Ephesians 5:20, "[Give] thanks always for all things to God the Father in the name of our Lord Jesus Christ" (NKJV). In 1789 George Washington declared that the fourth Thursday of every November was to be Thanksgiving Day in America. I say to you that the Word of God declares that every day ought to be a day of thanksgiving in the heart of every Christian.

Third, and finally, *gratitude is always to be expected.*

We are to give thanks in all things for "this is the will of God in Christ Jesus for you." I do not care what you are going through right now. I do not care what burdens you may be bearing or what trouble you might be in, if right now there is not a wellspring of thanksgiving boiling up out of your heart, you are out of the will of God. The only way to please God is to be obedient to his will. Now why does gratitude please our Lord so much?

It pleases God because *gratitude is the mark of a growing Christian*.

You see, gratitude is a real test of your character. For example, a baby is ungrateful. You can take a little baby when he has the colic and walk the floor with him for seven hours, and when you put that little baby down he won't look up at you and say, "Much obliged." He'll just yell a little louder. Now we don't blame him, because he's a baby.

Did you know that you have to teach a child to be grateful? Gratitude is not something that comes naturally. It's something you have to learn. You have to almost force children at times to say "Thank you." One lady gave her little grandson a piece of cake, and the little boy said, "Thank you." She said, "I love to hear little boys say thank you." He said, "Well, if you'll put ice cream on this cake I'll say it again." We expect that out of children.

But, friend, to continue to be ungrateful is to continue to be a baby. If you have no gratitude in your heart today, you simply show where you are spiritually. You may have the body of a giant and the mind of a Shakespeare, but you have the soul of a pygmy if you're not grateful.

Gratitude is the mark not only of the growing Christian, but of a *giving* Christian.

If for no other reason a Christian ought to give to the work of God. He ought to tithe his income to the Lord just out of gratitude of what God has given to him. I believe it is the height of ingratitude to a loving, giving God to refuse to give at least a tenth of your income back to him.

Everything you have is a gift from God. James 1:17 says, "Every good gift and every perfect gift is from above, and comes down from the Father of lights" (NKJV). If you are a grateful Christian, you will be a giving Christian.

Someone has well said, "Thanksgiving, to be truly thanksgiving, is first thanks, then giving." You can give without being thankful, but you cannot be thankful without giving. When you give, you are not only acknowledging that everything you have has been given to you by the Lord, but you are expressing your gratitude to him.

Gratitude is also the mark of a *glowing* Christian.

"It is good to give thanks to the LORD" (Ps. 92:1 NKJV). It is good to give thanks to the Lord. An attitude of gratitude will change your life. It will shield you from cynicism. It will keep you from criticism. It will protect you from pessimism. It will draw you close to God, and it will draw God close to you.

If you are unsaved, the best way to express your gratitude to the God who made you is to be saved. The psalmist said, "What shall I render unto the LORD for all his benefits?" Then he answers his own question, "I will take the cup of salvation, and call upon the name of the LORD" (Ps. 116:12, 13). If you will give your life to Jesus Christ, you will be eternally grateful that you did.

MOTHER'S DAY

10

Faith of Our Mothers

W. A. *Criswell*

2 *Timothy* 1:1–5

Paul, an apostle of Jesus Christ by the will of God, according to the promise of life which is in Christ Jesus, to Timothy, my dearly beloved son: Grace, mercy, and peace, from God the Father and Christ Jesus our Lord. I thank God, whom I serve from my forefathers with pure conscience, that without ceasing I have remembrance of thee in my prayers night and day; greatly desiring to see thee, being mindful of thy tears, that I may be filled with joy; when I call to remembrance the unfeigned faith that is in thee, which dwelt first in thy grandmother Lois, and thy mother Eunice; and I am persuaded that in thee also.

"*T*-E-L"—Timothy, Eunice, and Lois. A grandmother's class organized in many churches. The name came from this passage. Timothy the son, Eunice the mother, and Lois the grandmother.

I went one time to the Pacific Garden Mission in

Chicago. As I stood facing the pulpit, there to the right, engraved in block letters, they had painted "John 3:16." To the left, back of the pulpit against the wall, they had painted the question, "When last did you write to your mother?"

At first when I looked at them I thought how strange and even incongruous that there should be the great verse that summarizes the Holy Bible on this side, with that question, "When last did you write to your mother?" on the other side. Yet as I thought of it further I could easily see the inspiration that lay back of those two big writings. When a man came off of the street—a derelict, a piece of the flotsam and jetsam of discarded life—he would be down, almost destroyed. But as he came into that mission and saw the truth of John 3:16, he would have the opportunity to find the way of salvation. And that opportunity would be strengthened if he contemplated the faith of his mother. For the faith of our Christ and of the Bible is one so largely *shaped* and *fashioned* by her gracious hands. As the dipper holds and shapes the water, so our faith is so largely shaped by her.

In the book of Isaiah in chapter 51, the mighty prophet calls his people back to a *remembrance* of their fore-fathers. He says it like this, "Look to the rock from which you were hewn, / And to the hole of the pit from which you were dug. / Look to Abraham your father, / And to Sarah who bore you" (v. 1–2 NKJV). What a noble exhortation! For the beginning of the *chosen family* and race of God is found in the father and in the mother to whose remembrance Isaiah called the nation. It is so largely a story of Sarah and her son, Isaac, of Rebecca and her son Israel, and of Rachel and her beloved son, a type of Christ,

Joseph. Thus, it is a story, in the magnificent record of Genesis, of sons and their *mothers*.

It is no less true in the story of the founding and beginning of the *nation* itself. It is the work framed by a godly mother's hand. I do not know of a more unusual or impressive phenomenon in history than this: When Moses was the adopted son of Pharaoh's daughter and the heir-apparent to the crown, he made a great decision and chose rather to suffer with the people of God than to be exalted to the throne of the pharaohs. How could such a thing be? The story is laid bare before our eyes in the holy Scriptures.

When that little baby was retrieved from the bosom of the Nile River by the daughter of Pharaoh, she hired, unwittingly and unknowingly, the child's mother to raise up the little lad for her. And in the after-years when Moses was taught (for the Scriptures say "he was learned in all the arts and sciences and wisdom of the Egyptians") all of those books of idolatry and of darkened superstition, it could never be guessed what he would do with the knowledge. We know those writings in our time, for the texts have been recovered by archaeologists from the hermetically sealed sands of Egypt. We know the superstitions of those people, and we know the gods they worshiped— beasts and bugs. When Moses was taught all the idolatrous arts and sciences of the Egyptians, it seemed certain that he would be a devotee of that benighted and fiendish belief.

Yet when the time came in the prime of his life for the greatest decision a man could ever face, he chose the family and the people of God. Where did such a thing come from? And how could such a providence happen?

It is apparent that the mother who was hired to rear the lad for the daughter of Pharaoh also taught the boy, growing up as a small child, the faith of Jehovah God. And when the years multiplied and he came to the prime of life after the greatest decision he could face, he renounced the throne of the pharaohs that he might identify himself with the people of the Lord. Why? Because of a *woman*, a *mother* courageous and faithful to her God.

What was true in the beginning of the race of the chosen people, and at the beginning of the nation, nomadic before Egypt, was also the case in the beginning of the *prophets*. What is that story? It is a beautiful one that we read in the first and second chapters of 1 Samuel. It is the story of a *woman*, of Hannah and the little boy Samuel, whose name meant, "asked of God," whom she lent to the Lord all the days of his life.

It is no different in the story of the beginning of the *kings* of Israel. It begins in one of the most precious pastoral, idyllic romances to be found in human literature. It is the story of Ruth who reaped in the fields of Boaz and who became the mother of Obed, of Jesse, and of David. It is the story of a wonderful *woman*, a pagan Moabitess, who said to one of the daughters of Judah, "Entreat me not to leave thee, or to return from following after thee: for . . . thy people shall be my people, and thy God my God" (Ruth 1:16). This is the story of the beginning of the kingdom that shall last forever. It is the beginning of the throne of David.

Nor do you find any other departure from that paradigm and pattern in the life of *our Lord* in the New Testament evangelization of the world. The story begins, written by a beloved physician, as Paul called him, "Dr. Luke." It is the story of a mother, a woman. When you read it as Luke wrote it you easily sense that the story is told, poured out of the heart of Mary, the mother of our Lord. Thus, even the account of the culmination, the apex, the highest point of biblical revelation and of the fulfillment of the "hopes and fears of all the years" is the story of a *woman,* of a boy and his mother.

This one who began his life with the example of a faithful woman before him, saw the same pattern of faith in those he first encountered after being raised from the dead. The Easter account tells us not of the great faith of a Peter or a John. Immortalized and glorified, it is rather the story of a *woman,* the first to announce he was no longer among the dead, Mary Magdalene. And the first to greet him and salute him, risen Lord of all, was a group of women.

It is no less the same story in the *evangelization of the ancient world.* It began in Europe in a town named Philippi in a women's prayer meeting. There, in the home of Lydia, the first convert in Europe, the whole destiny of Western civilization was changed. It was in her home that Paul and his fellow companions lived as they preached the gospel of the grace of the Son of God. So, it was this *woman,* with magnanimous heart, redeemed by the blood of Jesus, who became the midwife of Western Christendom.

Beyond that only God in heaven knows how many times was the message of Christ introduced through a godly woman. The sainted apostle John, in his twilight years, in his second letter addresses in the first verse, "the elder unto the *elect lady* and her children." Who is that "elect lady"? Nobody knows. If you belong to the Eastern Star, one of those points is Electa, that is the name here, elect lady, in the Greek *electa*. Who she was, we do not know. But somewhere in the Greco-Roman world there was an introduction of the Christian faith in a pagan community, and it was through a godly mother and her children.

But if the Christian faith has been so largely shaped by mothers' hands it is no less so otherwise that *the Christian faith exalts her.* I want to show that by contrast. In the ancient world, the world of the Greek and the Roman, a woman was chattel, a piece of property. She was looked upon as no higher in status than a slave. Just as in many parts of Africa today, you buy a woman, you buy a wife for a goat. Or, if she is an unusually fine, attractive woman with a whole lot of brawn and muscle, she might bring a cow on the market. However, if she were unusually endued and endowed and could work twenty hours a day in the field as well as bear children that she carries on her back while she plows, she might be worth a cow and a calf. That is the ancient world's evaluation of the woman. Nor do you find any difference in most of the rest of the world.

Do you ever think about Greek culture and all of those marvelous things that come out of the genius of the Greek world and yet, unthinkably, their attitude toward the woman was of one of lowest valuation? The famous philosopher of Athens, Socrates, said, "Whatever gods there be, I thank the gods for three things. I thank the gods that I am a Greek and not a barbarian. I thank the gods that I am a free man and not a slave. And I thank the gods that I am a man and not a woman."

To be a woman was to be cursed in the ancient world.

And the religions outside the Christian faith are hardly any better. Mohammed had a vision from God, by which in the religion of Islam each man is limited to four wives at the same time. Mohammed himself had wives beyond count. But he had a vision limiting all of his followers to four wives. I once spoke with a Muslim merchant of the East. I asked the young man working by him, "How many wives does he have?"

He replied, "He just has two. But when he becomes more affluent he'll have four."

I responded, "How is it that you get along just limited to four wives?"

"That's simple," he answered. "By my religious faith, I cannot have but four at the same time. But, when I find another I wish to marry, I just get rid of one of those four and then I get that other woman. I always keep it at four."

"Well," I said, "how do you divorce one of your wives?"

"I just tell one of them that she must leave. Then I bring in the other wife."

"It's that simple?" I asked.

"Yes, it's that simple. I've been doing that for many years."

That is the theology of the value of womanhood in the eye of a Muslim devotee. You wouldn't find anything different if you went to visit the Hindus, and there are hundreds of millions of Hindus in the Eastern world. I have watched those people starve to death, and it is not hard to understand why India starves to death. The attitudes they have toward the animal world and the attitudes they have toward the woman are completely contrary to the teaching of the Word of God. Their basic doctrine is the transmigration of the soul. That is, when you die you come back in another form. This is what they believe: If you've been bad in this life you'll come back as a monkey. If you've been really bad in this life, you'll come back as a black spider. But if you have been abominable in this life you'll be really cursed; you'll come back as a woman.

Christianity *exalted woman*. It was to a *woman* that God revealed that this child is the Messiah who was promised. Her name was Anna.

It was to a *woman* that the Lord spoke, even an unspeakable woman, when he revealed his messianic identity in the fourth chapter of John, and spoke to her the greatest sermon ever delivered on spiritual worship. It was to her that he preached that God wanted those who worship him to do so in spirit and in truth.

It was to a *woman* that the Lord called the attention of the apostles, and said, "Look at her; she has given more than they all. She dropped into the treasury of the Lord all of her living, just trusting God."

It was for a *woman* that the Lord stopped the funeral procession in Nain and gave back into her arms her only son.

It was for a *woman* that Christ raised her brother from the dead. Later, when she anointed him and wiped his feet with the hair of her head, it was for a *woman* he said, "As long as this gospel is preached this should be told as a memorial for her." I am helping to fulfill that prophecy this sacred hour.

It was for a *woman* that the Lord stopped his dying for our sins and said to the apostle John, "John, look at your mother, she is your mother; from now on take care of her;

and mother, this is your son." From that moment on the apostle John took her into his own home and cared for her.

It would be impossible to dissociate the faith of our mothers from the faith of the Lord Jesus Christ.

> Faith of our mothers, guiding faith
> For youthful longings struggled in doubt.
> How blurred our vision how blind our way
> Thy providence of care without.
>
> Faith of our mothers, guiding faith,
> We will be true to thee till death.
> Faith of our mothers, Christian faith
> In truth beyond our man-made creeds
>
> Still serve the home and save the church.
> And breathe thy spirit through our deeds.
> Faith of our mothers, Christian faith,
> We will be true to thee till death.

This is the commitment of my heart forever. This is the commitment of the heart of millions in God's presence in churches all over this land today. May we all pause and thank God today for our mothers.

FATHER'S DAY

11

"Hi Dad, 'Bye Dad"

Ed Young

Proverbs 22:6

Train up a child in the way he should go: and when he is old, he will not depart from it.

*E*very sixty seconds in America one hundred twenty-five young people see their parents get divorced. One hundred and seven children are born out of wedlock to teenage mothers. One hundred and thirty-seven run away from home. Seventy-seven children are abused and neglected. Sixty-six teenagers drop out of school. Eighteen are arrested for drinking or drunken driving. Nine are arrested for drug abuse. One hundred and seventeen get pregnant. Three hundred twenty-three teenagers become sexually active. Forty-six teenagers have an abortion. Twenty-six contract syphilis or gonorrhea. Every ninety seconds a teenager attempts to take his own life; every ninety minutes he succeeds. Fifty percent of all high school seniors are sexually active. Fifty percent of all high school seniors have used marijuana. Ninety percent of all high school seniors have used alcohol.

Statistics, general statistics: What do they mean? I don't think you have to be a rocket scientist to see that this generation of young people in America is in serious trouble. It didn't happen overnight. This decade is a little worse than the last decade, and the last decade was a little worse than the decade before that.

We need to ask this very profound question on Father's Day: What has gone wrong? What has changed in our society? What leads so many young people today to get into serious trouble? There are many answers. But all the surveys, all the studies, all the polls keep pointing to one tremendous factor—the absence of a male influence in the home. I believe that is the root cause of the epidemic of problems today among our young people. So, we look around and say, "It's the man." It's you, sir. It's you, young man. It's me. It's the men. Oh, there are other causes. But when you look at all the broken lives, all the suffering, all the problems, all the drug abuse and so on it is clear that our problems are complex, and that no single culprit can be assigned for every ill. But I am still convinced that the key to the maze is to be found right here.

It is obvious that our society has a very negative view of men. There's a reason for that. It's because men have not been there in the home. Divorce devastates children. Make no mistake about it. Clearly, not every home has been ravaged by divorce. But know this: A husband who does not divorce his mate but spends very little time in the home with the children frustrates the young people. This is where we are in our land today. Nearly half the homes in America have nonresident fathers; a large percentage of the rest have virtually absentee fathers. It is little wonder we're in such a terrible condition.

The Bible clearly says that the male is to be the spiritual leader in the home, but most men have long ago abdicated that responsibility. If there is to be spiritual training and nurture we usually have the attitude that the wife should do it, the mother should do it. Thank God, they often do, or it wouldn't get done at all. But in the average home in America, this verse of Scripture has been virtually forgotten.

Now, what does it mean to train up a child in the way he should go? Does it mean I take my children and I train them up in the way I believe they should go? Not at all. It means that my role as a father, as a spiritual leader of my home is to train up the children in the way *they* should go. That phrase has to do with the way they are *bent*. It concerns the way that their lives are naturally pointed, the way that God has pointed them. So we as spiritual leaders, gentlemen, are to get in on what God is doing in the lives of our children. We are to take part in helping God and helping those children be pointed in the way that God Almighty wants them to go. In other words, it's not what *I want*, it's not what *I like,* not the frustrated ambitions *I feel* about the life of my child that is the first issue here. No! We have a responsibility to know and understand the character, the gifts, and the abilities of our child, so that we can ascertain, under the direction of God's Spirit, his bent, his strengths. When we have discovered *that,* we can create a nurturing, spiritual environment that will enable that child to go the way God wants him to go, to discover for himself God's direction and purpose for his life.

Here we are today, Father's Day. Here we are making all kinds of analyses of what's wrong with our young people, our boys and girls, our homes, and the conclusion continually takes us right back to Dad. Something is wrong with the males in our society. Desperately wrong!

In a discussion session in our church, teenagers were asked, "When we say the word *father* what comes to your mind?" One teenager responded, "Hi Dad, 'bye Dad." That sums it up for many, doesn't it? That's about the extent of the conversation many fathers have with their children. It's just doorway talk, on the way in or on the way out. There are too many "Hi Dad, 'bye Dad" dads in our society. Now I want to ask you a question. Are you a "Hi Dad, 'bye Dad"? When you hear a story like that, do you begin to wonder if it was your child who gave that assessment? Do you have a *real* relationship, Dad, with your son, with your daughter? Do you have a *genuine* relationship with your children? Or are you just another one of those "Hi Dad, 'bye Dad" kind of daddies?

Now where does training children begin? It begins with the male's relationship with the female, with the dad's relationship to the mother. The best training you'll ever give to your children in every realm of development is the training they get by observing your love for their mother and the relationship the two of you have in the home.

Now there are *seven factors,* gentlemen, that need to be operating in your life and in my life and our relationship with our mates. These factors can be stumbling blocks. But a *stumbling block* can be a *stepping-stone.* The same stone you and I can stumble over can be a stone we can step on that helps us to walk and get through a certain boggy area. These seven factors could also be called the seven deadly concerns of women about their men. You could take a survey today of the concerns of all the wives and mothers in this worship service and you'd put together a list that is pretty close to the one I'm about to give. This is what women say about you; this is what women say about me.

First, Dad, Husband *be tender!* That's hard for some men. Be tender toward your wife. She is a delicate, precious person. Be tender. Be ready and eager to say, "I love you." Be tender. Your children need to see this in you.

Second, *be courteous!* I know men who are so gracious and so kind and so hospitable, in public. But when they get with their wives it is obvious that they are kinder to a perfect stranger, someone they will never see again, than they are in the family relationship to their lifetime mate and to their children. Husband, Dad, be courteous!

Third, *be entertaining!* Some of you guys will bore your wives to death. Boy, you're out in public, "Hey, how are you doing? I got a good story I'll tell you about the office; I'm excited about this and that." I know men who are just a lot of fun to be with, but their wives say that at home they are a drag! Be entertaining! Have fun!

Fourth, *be patient!* This is going to come as a shock to some of you men: Women are different from you. Every month, the physiologists tell us, they go through cycles in a different way than men. They think differently than we think. They operate differently than we operate. Their world view is somewhat different from ours. Be patient! This is so important! If you demonstrate patience toward your wife, your sons and daughters will learn patience also.

Fifth, *be fair* to your wife in *money matters!* I know a man very well who has a real problem with this matter of money spent in the home. He's got plenty of money to buy shotguns, to go on hunting trips, to go to athletic events. He flies across the country. He's got plenty of money, but at home with his wife he is constantly carping about her expenditures, "Make the children's clothes! We can't afford to buy anything." He's spending thousands of dollars on his own recreation, on his own habits, and on his own dress. But he makes his wife pinch pennies. Be fair in financial matters!

Sixth, *be truthful!* It is hard to love somebody who doesn't tell you the truth. If your wife is married to somebody she cannot trust, life for her will become unbearable. Be truthful! There is a crisis of truth-telling among young people today, and one of the main reasons is that fathers don't always tell the truth to their wives.

Finally, the one negative item in the list. I think it's important. All women mention it. *Don't use your wife as a scapegoat in conversation with friends and other people!* If you're always putting her down, belittling her, it can hurt her deeply. The same is true for your children. Build them up; don't tear them down. There's not usually anything wrong with a little lighthearted needling, but for some men it's a constant barrage. It's almost vogue to do this in our society today, men. We have to be very careful at this point. What begins as humor sometimes degenerates to a mean-spirited verbal assault.

These are the seven things that can be either stepping-stones or stumbling blocks. How you treat your spouse in these areas will speak volumes to your kids. Be tender. Be courteous. Have fun in your home. Be patient. Be fair about money matters. Be truthful. Don't be cutting and sarcastic with your mate. Seven things. That's where we begin to teach our children.

Now let's flip it over and talk about what we are to impart to our children. What do we teach? First of all, I think we teach them that *life is exciting* and not just something to be endured. You don't just "get through" life; *be enthusiastic about it!* Life is exciting. We need to teach our children expectation. Teach them to have a positive expectation for tomorrow.

It takes time to teach children to be enthusiastic. Those children in the New Testament came running to Jesus. What did the apostles do? "Hey, you boys and girls, step back; he's a busy man. He doesn't have time for you. Man, this is the Messiah, this is the Son of God. He's going to be around just thirty-three years. You boys and girls get back; he's got a big agenda." What did Jesus say? "Suffer the little children to come unto me." He said all the crowds and the healing and the teaching and preaching could wait. He was interested in children. Let the little children come.

Do you have time for your children? Most men substitute money for time. They say, "Hey, I'm out here working. I'm making money. I'm going to buy you this. I'm going to give you that. You can have these things. I'll buy you whatever you want, but I just don't have time to go to your game. I don't have the time to sit down and talk." We are more willing to spend money than we are to spend time.

I saw a cartoon that showed a dad busy at home working. The mother was busy, and their little boy turned around and was looking right straight "at the camera," saying, "I'm always getting a busy signal at home." How many times do we put our children on hold? We give them the busy signal. We become experts at putting our children off. We say, "We have plenty of time for you. We'll do it tomorrow," or "Daddy's tired." Wives get tired too, Dad. It is staggering that some men never realize that their wives get tired too! "Dad, play with me!" "Oh, son, I'm tired." "Dad, what do you think about this?" "Oh, I'm sorry, I have to make a phone call." We give our kids a busy signal.

Do you know what will happen if you give your kids a busy signal too often? They will start dialing other numbers. Then one day you'll say, "I don't know about Suzy or Billy. I asked them to come with me and have some fun, but they weren't interested in it anymore. They didn't want to go, and I had to make them." You see, if you put them on hold and give them those busy signals long enough, they will begin dialing other numbers. They'll move on. Teach them to be enthusiastic about life! That's the role of a father. That's what Jesus did. "Suffer the little children to come unto me."

Also we need to teach them to be *dependent*. Notice, I said dependent, not *in*dependent. We get it backward. A father says, "I want to teach you to be independent, son. I want you to be a success in life. I want you to stand on your own two feet. This world doesn't owe you a living. I want you to reach those goals." We teach them that, and there's a certain value in it. It's important. But we also need to teach them to be dependent.

A young child is dependent. "Tie my shoe. Open the

door. Help me with this. Guide me over here." We need to teach them to be dependent. We need to let them know they can come to us with any need, any question, and that they'll always find us willing to help.

I know a dad who prides himself when his son or daughter asks a question. He answers that question thoroughly, to the "nth degree." One day his boy asked him, "Dad, where does water come from?"

He said, "Come on, son, I'll show you."

He took him to the bathroom and turned on the spigot. He told him water comes out of here. He showed him the pipes. He explained the mechanics of valves and pressure inside the house. Then they went down and looked under the house. "See the pipe? It goes into the ground. Come on, son."

They walked to the yard to the water meter, and the dad explained the meter process. "The water comes through a large pipe under the street. Get in the car; I want to show you."

They followed the pipeline all the way down the street until they arrived at the purifying plant. "This is where our water comes from. This is how they purify the water." He showed him the filters, and how the process worked. Then they got back in the car. "There's the water tower. It's up on a hill. That's how we get pressure in our lines."

Then they drove to the reservoir outside town. "The water comes from the lake, to the plant, to the tower. Of course, the water for this lake comes from clouds as God blesses us with rainfall."

By the time he was done, that child had an education. (Very likely some of you here have too!) What kind of child do you think that child became? He became a very *thorough* child, who in any academic situation goes right to the bottom line of every question he is asked. Why? Because Daddy made time to thoroughly answer the questions he asked.

That's a father; that's a daddy. That's not just a parent or a male. We must teach our children to be dependent. Tell them it's all right to ask questions, even foolish questions, silly questions. Children asked Jesus questions all the time. Jesus answered. Jesus heard. Jesus had time. Teach them it's all right to be dependent.

Then, finally the father needs to teach the child to *trust!* An atheist lifted his seven-year-old son onto a countertop. "Jump down. Your daddy will catch you," he instructed the boy. The little guy jumped, but the father pulled back his arms and the little guy crash-landed. The father said, "The sooner you learn that's the way it is in life, the better off you'll be."

I want you to know today: That's a lie! We need to teach our children to trust their father, to trust what happens in their home. If they jump they need to be assured that Daddy is there ready enthusiastically to catch them. That's the way they learn that there are also everlasting arms there to catch them every time they fall. Daddies, teach your children to trust you, and they will have an easier time learning to trust God.

What kind of dad are you? Are you a "Hi Dad, 'bye Dad"? Or are you a dad who has the right relationship with your mate? Are you a dad who is enthusiastic about life? Are you teaching your children to be enthusiastic about life and to be dependent in the right way? Are you teaching them to trust in the benevolent, loving intentions of their earthly father, and so to learn to be confident in the trustworthiness of the Savior of the world?

What's wrong with our society? There are too many "Hi Dad, 'bye Dad" dads. Every Father's Day I try to read this. It is a familiar song, but it has a tremendous message:

My child arrived just the other day.
He came into the world in the usual way.
But there were planes to catch and bills to pay.
He learned to walk while I was away.
And he was talking before I knew
And as he grew he said
"I'm going to be like you, Dad,
You know I'm going to be like you?"

And the cat's in the cradle and the silver spoon
The little boy blue and the man in the moon.
"When you coming home Dad?"
"I don't know when, but we"ll get together then, son,
You know we"ll have a good time then."

My son turned ten just the other day, he said
"Thanks for the ball, Dad, come on let's play
Can you teach me to throw?" I said "Not today
I got a lot to do." He said "That's okay."
And he walked away, but his smile never dimmed
He said, "I'm going to be like him,
You know I'm gonna be like him."

And the cat's in the cradle and the silver spoon
The little boy blue and the man on the moon.
When you coming home, dad?

I don't know when, but we'll get together then, son
You know we'll have a good time then.

Well he came home from college just the other day.
So much a man I just had to say,
"Son, I'm proud of you can't you sit for awhile?"
He shook his head and said with a smile
"What I'd really like Dad is to borrow the car keys,
See ya later can I have them please?"

And the cat's in the cradle and the silver spoon
The little boy blue and the man on the moon.
When you coming home, Dad? I don't know when
But we'll have a good time then, son
You know we'll have a good time then.

I've long since retired my son has moved away.
I called him up just the other day.
I said, "Son, I'd like to see you if you don't mind."
He said "I'd love to Dad if I could find the time.
You see my new job's a hassle and kids have the flu
But it's sure nice talking to you, Dad,
It's been sure nice talking to you."

And as I hung up the phone it occurred to me
He'd grown up just like me, my boy was just like me.

And the cat's in the cradle and the silver spoon
Little boy blue and the man on the moon
When you coming home, son? I don't when
But we'll get together then, Dad,
You know we'll have a good time then.

"Hi Dad, 'bye Dad": one of our greatest problems today.

INDEPENDENCE DAY

12

Why the Friendship of God Keeps Us Free

Artis Fletcher

T *James 2:2–16*

he thirteen original American colonies did not want to submit to the taxation and other demands of Great Britain. A series of events and meetings led us to declare, on July 4, 1776, our independence from Great Britain; this declaration was followed by the Revolutionary War.

For over two hundred years God has blessed us as a nation to remain free, in part because of his grace and mercy and also because we have done some things, as a nation, that have caused God to smile on us. We, as a nation, should continue to seek God's place of blessing. We can only remain free and be in the place of blessing if we will, as a people and as a nation, seek the will of God. God says to us in his Word that righteousness exalts a nation, but sin is a reproach to any people.

I will not attempt to cover all of the things we have done that have allowed us to remain in favor with God, but I would like to deal with a few of what I believe to be "key" things.

First, we have been a friend to Israel. "I will bless those who bless you, and whoever curses you I will curse; and all peoples on earth will be blessed through you" (Gen. 12:3 NIV).

The word *bless* used in this passage means to bless God as an act of adoration and to bless man as a benefit. This suggests to us that our friendship toward Israel is tied to our friendship toward God. Based on God's sovereignty he chose Abraham and made of him a great nation and promised his blessings upon Abraham and the nation. Throughout the generations, those who have obeyed this principle in Genesis 12:3 have been blessed by God. I believe one of the reasons we have prospered as a nation is that we have not, as a nation, oppressed the chosen people of God.

Based on the meaning of the word *bless* in verse 3 we bless God by blessing Israel, which in turn provokes the blessings of God upon us. Based on God's Word, one of the things that could hurt us as a nation and move us out of the place of favor with him is for us to curse Israel; if we do this, God promises to curse us. The word that he uses for "curse" also means to "bitterly curse." Examples of how God can bitterly curse a nation that seeks to curse Israel are found throughout the scriptures. Psalm 137 records the cruelty of the Edomites as they joined Nebuchadnezzar in his siege of Jerusalem. They continue from their beginning as descendants of Esau to oppose Israel until they eventually disappear from the pages of history, leaving only the city of Petra, the Rose Red City, which has its place in biblical prophecy. When you are annihilated from the face of the earth, and you disappear from the pages of history, you have been bitterly cursed by God. We have taken, as a nation, much criticism from those within and those without for blessing God's chosen people. But if you understand the mandate of Scripture you will be opposing God when you curse his chosen people. One of the reasons I say again that we have remained a free and blessed nation for these two hundred-plus years is that we have been friendly to God's chosen people.

Second, we have been a friend to the poor.

The word *poor* means to be destitute, to lack, to be needy. As a nation and as a people historically we have been friendly toward the poor. Enough of us have been sensitive to biblical mandates to raise the conscience of the nation, so we would be sympathetic toward the poor. According to Proverbs 14:31, "He who oppresses the poor shows contempt for their Maker, but whoever is kind to the needy honors God" (NIV). Honoring God means to glorify him, and when we honor and glorify him he wants to bless us.

He who mocks the poor shows contempt for their Maker.
(Prov. 17:5*a* NIV)

He who is kind to the poor lends to the LORD, and he will reward him for what he has done.
(Prov. 19:17 NIV)

The word *lend* implies a form of obligation, an abiding with, a cleaving or joining. Because we recognize that we are obligated to the poor, we cleave to the poor, we join the poor, lend to the poor; we are actually then lending to the Lord, according to Proverbs 19:17. And that which has been given, he will pay again; that which we give to the poor, when we help them, the Lord promises to pay us back.

In James 1:27 the test of whether our religion is pure and undefiled before God the Father is based on our treatment of the fatherless and widows in their affliction. We live in a busy world, and we are involved in many activities. But it is a blessing and a joy when we will take the time and put our priorities in order so we can visit the orphans and the widows in their affliction.

James also warns us in James 5:4 that we should be careful not to defraud the poor. When we hire someone who is poor to do some work for us, we should have a clear understanding with them before the work is done. It should be understood when and how much we will pay them. Do you realize that refusing to pay the poor worker at the time we agreed to pay him constitutes fraud? It incites the anger of the Lord against us and can cause his judgment to come upon us. James 5:4 says:

> Behold, the hire of the labourers who have reaped down your fields, which is of you kept back by fraud, crieth: and the cries of them which have reaped are entered into the ears of the Lord of sabaoth.

James is saying that by our mistreatment of the poor we are causing God to hear something that he should not hear.

Sometimes even church folk will be guilty of working the poor and withholding their Social Security and other benefits that they rightly deserve. I know a man who worked many years for his employer doing construction work. He can walk around in the small community where he lives today and point out home after home where he mixed every drop of mortar that was used in the building. He can point out stores, factories, and other businesses and reminisce about the days he mixed mortar for them and how the block and brick layers never had to wait for the mortar. During all these years his employer withheld Social Security from his check. When he retired and it was time for him to receive his Social Security, none had been paid for him. He had been defrauded. Yet, he relied on Romans 12:19: "Do not take revenge, my friends, but leave room for God's wrath, for it is written: 'It is mine to avenge; I will repay,' says the Lord" (NIV). Others encouraged him to sue, or turn his employer over to the authorities, but he did not. He did not take it to the authorities, but the matter has come before the Final Authority. It has been heard by the "Lord of sabaoth." The word *sabaoth* is used only twice in the Bible, in James 5:4 and Romans 9:29. It means "armies" and is a military epithet of God. This is saying to us that when we defraud the poor we disturb and summon the armies of God for our destruction.

James instructs us on how to act toward the poor in our assemblies in the following verses:

> Suppose a man comes into your meeting wearing a gold ring and fine clothes, and a poor man in shabby clothes also comes in. If you show special attention to the man wearing fine clothes and say, "Here's a good seat for you," but say to the poor man, "You stand there" or "Sit on the floor by my feet," have you not discriminated among yourselves and become judges with evil thoughts?
>
> Listen, my dear brothers: Has not God chosen those

who are poor in the eyes of the world to be rich in faith and to inherit the kingdom he promised those who love him? But you have insulted the poor. Is it not the rich who are exploiting you? Are they not the ones who are dragging you into court? Are they not the ones who are slandering the noble name of him to whom you belong?

If you really keep the royal law found in Scripture, "Love your neighbor as yourself," you are doing right. But if you show favoritism, you sin and are convicted by the law as lawbreakers.... If one of you says to him, "Go, I wish you well; keep warm and well fed," but does nothing about his physical needs, what good is it?

(James 2:2–9, 16 NIV)

Everyone, whether in a suit and tie or faded jeans and a T-shirt, should be welcome in our assembly.

My nephew, who lives in Chicago, on one occasion came to visit our church. He shared with me how he had begun to go to church and how excited he was that he was in a church where he was not judged by the way he was dressed. He continued to share with me about how the pastor of his church had gone out into the community and took a survey of the people who did not come to church. Many of them said they did not go to church because they did not feel like "dressing up."

The pastor then welcomed the people with their casual dress, and some came to church, were saved, and discipled. As he shared his testimony with me, I thought about how ironic it was that the ones with the mission to draw people to Jesus have often set up unbiblical standards that alienate people from the Savior.

The fact of the matter is that the church should show

some latitude and flexibility in reaching out to the lost. If persons should come into our midst who are not dressed according to "our standards" because of poverty, we should not ask them to sit in a corner and make them feel unwelcome. Remember that one of the reasons God has smiled on us as a nation for over two hundred years is because we have been friendly to the poor.

We must also remember that we can learn from the poor. James says in verse 5 that the poor are rich in faith. We can benefit from having the poor in our midst because they can teach us how to believe in God. In order to keep God's smile on us we should not be respecters of persons. When we do this we commit sin and become transgressors of the law (James 2:9). If we are unwilling to respond to the needs of the poor with real help rather than just lip service, James asks us in verse 16, "What does it profit?" He is not only asking "What does it profit the poor?" He is also asking, "What does it profit you?" We can actually profit and have the favor of God on our lives, family, and country by being friendly to the poor.

Third, our nation has been a friend to politics.

Human government emerges on the pages of history from the Word of God. He established and ordained government shortly after the flood, for he says in Genesis 9:6: "Whoever sheds the blood of man, / by man shall his blood be shed; / for in the image of God / has God made man" (NIV). "The highest function of government is the judicial taking of life. All other governmental powers are implied in that."[1] In the light of the fact that human government was established by God, Jesus says to us in Mark

12:17a: "Render to Caesar the things that are Caesar's, and to God the things that are God's."

The apostle Paul picks up the idea in Romans 13 that the government officials are ordained of God. We as Christians must recognize that respect for human government is a spiritual matter. Thank God, many of the government officials are Christians and members of our churches. As they go into the arena of politics armed with the *principles* of God and filled with the *Spirit* of God we can have a political position that is sensitive to the *will* and *plan* of God, which will continue to invoke the *blessings* of God upon our nation.

I know the prophets of doom have predicted our downfall, but we have done some good things. For example, we risked life and limb in criticism to go to the aid of the people in Kuwait when they were being trampled by a more powerful enemy. We said by those actions that God is on the side of justice and we are seeking to be his representatives. We again risked life and limb and political criticism to go to Somalia and confront the warlords and make food available to the starving and medical care available to the sick. We are also using our influence in Bosnia and other countries to try to establish a fair and just political system. I believe if we, as a nation, seek God more and seek to follow him, do what is just and right, he will allow us to remain an independent and free nation for years to come.

Many people believe that politics is evil and that Christians should not be involved. Many believe that we should be committed to God, love him, and leave politics alone. But remember, politics determines what our children learn, how the poor are treated, jobs, wages, and many other matters of justice in this world. Because of the way politics is woven into the very fiber of our society it is very important that Christianity be the *conscience* of politics. By so doing we can continue as a free nation, and we can continue to be an example for other nations to follow.

According to *World Book Encyclopedia,* the Declaration of Independence is so profound that many nations have received inspiration and guidance from it as they have sought freedom and independence from foreign rule. If we continue with a remnant as a nation to follow the principles and precepts of God we will be a light, a beacon, and an example by the grace of God. It is still righteousness that exalts a nation, and sin is a reproach to any people.

Finally, we have been a friend to religion.

The Declaration of Independence grew out of hostile and difficult times in the birth of a nation. When you read the Declaration of Independence today, it is clear that there was a great deal of oppression. King George III of Britain imposed taxes without consent, and deprived the citizens in many cases of the benefit of trial by jury. The Declaration of Independence says he took away our character, abolished our valuable laws and altered the most fundamental forms of government, suspended our legislators, plundered the high seas, ravished the coastlines, burned the towns, and destroyed the lives of people. "He has constrained our fellow Citizens taken Captive on the high Seas to bear Arms against their Country, to become the executioners of their friends and Brethren, or to fall themselves by their Hands.

"He has excited domestic insurrections amongst us, and has endeavored to bring on the inhabitants of our frontiers the merciless Indian Savages, whose known rule of warfare, is an undistinguished destruction of all ages, sexes and conditions."

These conditions unsettled the family and community so that the freedom of religion was jeopardized. They removed from the citizens the same privileges that we enjoy today, such as the right to worship our God in peace and safety. There was no such thing in that day as respect for the principles that are now set forth in the First Amendment of the Constitution, which reads:

> Congress shall make no law respecting an establishment of religion, or prohibiting the free exercise thereof; or abridging the freedom of speech, or of the press; or the right of the people peaceably to assemble, and to petition the Government for a redress of grievances.

This amendment to the Constitution (which did not exist in the days before the Declaration of Independence) assures us that the days that existed before the Declaration of Independence will not come again. As proclaimers of the Word of God we should train our people, which may include many legislators, to always protect our rights to freedom of religion. We should be thankful to God for his continuous blessings upon us to have the freedom and protection of the law and to worship God when and as we please.

We have the right, as Jesus said, to render to God that which is his: worship, praise, and adoration. We also have the right to carry out the Great Commission, which is to make disciples (Matt. 28:19–20). The worshiping of God, the making of disciples, the support of missions, and ministry to the poor are primary responsibilities that God has given to us. Our freedom of religion guarantees our right to carry out these God-given responsibilities. If we reduce our freedom of religion to simply *having* church, rather than *being* the church and *carrying out* our God-given mission, God is not responsible for still holding the doors of the freedom of religion open to us. The church will become like an unused muscle of the body that loses its ability to function.

On this blessed day of independence, I hope we have had occasion to remember. I hope we have remembered that we have done some things right and that God has smiled on us as a nation. First, we have been a friend to Israel. Second, we have been a friend to the poor. Third, we have been a friend to politics. Fourth, we have been a friend to religion. These are some of the reasons why at this time of independence we can praise God for smiling on us. You cannot effectively praise him, however, if you do not know him personally. The way you come to know him personally is as simple as A-B-C:

Admit your sin to God and recognize your inability to save yourself (Rom. 3:23; Titus 3:5).

Believe that God loves you and that Christ died in your place (John 3:16; 1 Peter 3:18).

Call on the Lord Jesus to save you, and receive him as your personal Savior (Rom. 10:13; John 1:12).

Won't you do it today?

Notes

Preface
1. D. Martyn Lloyd-Jones, *Preaching and Preachers* (Grand Rapids: Zondervan, 1971), 191–92.

Chapter 2
1. William Hendricksen, *New Testament Commentary: Pastoral Epistles* (Grand Rapids: Baker, 1957).

Chapter 5
1. Walter Kaiser, *Toward an Old Testament Theology* (Grand Rapids: Zondervan, 1978), 20–40.
2. Jean Danielou, *Origen,* trans. Walter Mitchell (New York: Sheed and Ward, 1955), 271.

Chapter 12
1. Notes on Genesis 8:21, *The New Scofield Reference Bible* (Oxford: Oxford University Press, 1967).

Contributors

John Bisagno is pastor of the 22,000-member First Baptist Church of Houston, where he has served since 1970. Previously he pastored the First Southern Baptist Church of Del City, Oklahoma. He has written several books, including *How to Build an Evangelistic Church*.

Stuart Briscoe has been pastor of the Elmbrook Church in Brookfield, Wisconsin, since 1970. The church has a weekly attendance of over 6,000. A native of England, he and his wife, Jill, served with the youth organization Torchbearers for several years. He is author of many books.

W. A. Criswell is Senior Pastor, Emeritus, of the First Baptist Church of Dallas. He is a world-renowned preacher and author of over fifty books.

Artis Fletcher is Senior Pastor of the Mendenhall Bible Church in Mendenhall, Mississippi, where he has served since 1975. He is a graduate of Los Angeles Baptist Theological Seminary.

Jack Graham is pastor of the Prestonwood Baptist Church in Dallas, Texas. He has pastored five other churches, including the First Baptist Church of West Palm Beach, Florida. His weekly television ministry is available to 19 million homes on the ACTS network. He holds a doctorate from Southwestern Baptist Theological Seminary in Fort Worth.

Jack Hayford is Senior Pastor of the Church on the Way, Van Nuys, California. He has served that congregation since 1969. He is author of twenty-six books and over 400 songs and hymns, including the chorus "Majesty." He holds a doctorate from Oral Roberts University.

D. James Kennedy is pastor of the Coral Ridge Presbyterian Church in Fort Lauderdale, Florida. He is President and Founder of Evangelism Explosion, which trains laypersons in evangelism in ninety-three nations throughout the world.

James Merritt is pastor of the First Baptist Church, Snellville, Georgia, which is in the Greater Atlanta area. He previously pastored three other churches and holds the Ph.D. degree from the Southern Baptist Theological Seminary.

Calvin Miller is Professor of Communications and Evangelism at the Southwestern Baptist Theological Seminary in Ft. Worth, Texas. He was a pastor for many years, and is author of numerous books, including *The Singer Trilogy* and *Spirit, Word, and Story.* He is a frequent conference speaker.

Stephen Olford is Founder of Encounter Ministries and the Institute for Biblical Preaching, both of which are in Memphis, Tennessee. He has pastored churches in England and the United States and is one of the foremost conference speakers in America.

Jay Strack is one of the most widely known evangelists in America. He preaches to over a million people annually and has written many books, including *Good Kids Who Do Bad Things*.

Ed Young is pastor of the Second Baptist Church of Houston, Texas. He is a graduate of Southeastern Baptist Theological Seminary and was President of the Southern Baptist Convention, 1992–1994.